EUROPEAN TRAVELLERS IN INDIA

EUROPEAN TRAVELLERS IN INDIA

During the Fifteenth, Sixteenth and Seventeenth Centuries, the Evidence afforded by them with respect to Indian Social Institutions and the Nature and Influence of Indian Governments

E F Oaten

Low Price Publications
2015

First Published 1909
Reprinted in **LPP** 2000, 2010, 2015

ISBN 10: 81-7536-508-0
ISBN 13: 978-81-7536-508-7

Published by
Low Price Publications
A-6, 2nd Floor, Nimri Commercial Centre,
Ashok Vihar Phase 4, Delhi 110052 (INDIA)
tel.: +91-11-27302453 fax.: +91-11-47061936
url: www.LPPindia.com e-mail: info@LPPindia.com

Printed at
Balaji Offset, Delhi

PRINTED IN INDIA

EUROPEAN TRAVELLERS IN INDIA

DURING THE FIFTEENTH, SIXTEENTH AND SEVENTEENTH CENTURIES; THE EVIDENCE AFFORDED BY THEM WITH RESPECT TO INDIAN SOCIAL INSTITUTIONS, & THE NATURE & INFLUENCE *of* INDIAN GOVERNMENTS

by EDW[D] FARLEY OATEN, B.A., LL.B., *late* SCHOLAR *of* SIDNEY SUSSEX COLLEGE, CAMBRIDGE

KEGAN PAUL TRENCH TRÜBNER AND COMPANY LIMITED · DRYDEN HOUSE · GERRARD St LONDON W 1909

To

My Sister Etheline

We were dreamers, dreaming greatly. . . .
We yearned beyond the sky-line where
the strange roads go down.
Came the Whisper, came the Vision. . . .

RUDYARD KIPLING.

PREFACE

THE subject for the Le Bas Prize Essay of 1908 was as follows: "European travellers in India during the fifteenth, sixteenth, and seventeenth centuries; the evidence afforded by them with respect to Indian social institutions, and the nature and influence of Indian Governments."

It is obvious that more than one method of approaching this subject was possible. A careful dissection and analysis of the travellers' narratives, regarding them as soulless depositories of facts rather than as human documents, would, doubtless, have been by no means devoid of value. This style of treatment, however, was open to two serious objections. It precluded all but the slightest mention of travellers who were not writers, or whose writings have perished; and it reduced a picturesque collection of romantic yarns to the level of an unimaginative, monkish chronicle. "To the ende," however (if I may quote Richard Hakluyt), "that those men which were the payneful and personall travellers might reape that good opinion and just commendation which they have deserved," I have adopted an opposite mode of treatment. I have striven throughout to regard the various characters who flit across the following pages in the light as much of adventurers and pioneers as of collectors of social and political facts—in other words, I have tried to preserve in my narrative as much as I could of the large amount of human interest which naturally invests the subject, and animates the writings, of these early wanderers in India. Such an attitude, which permits the discussion of men who travelled, but left no record, made the definition of the word "traveller," for the purposes of this essay, a matter of great difficulty, and necessitated the drawing of an arbitrary line of distinction between the "traveller" and the adventurer who cannot be termed such. The principle of this distinction will be found fully explained in the first chapter, and, though, as there stated, I have deviated from it on occasion, it will be found to have decided most doubtful claims to inclusion.

A few remarks are necessary on the subject of the orthography of Indian names. In quotations the original spelling has been followed, whether it be the crude "Jno. Gernaet" of the seventeenth-century traveller, or the diacritical exactness of the Indian Text Series. In the other parts of the essay I have not thought it worth while to adopt an elaborate system, but have aimed at simplicity, at the same time shunning uncouth forms, and avoiding inconsistencies as far as possible. That I have not entirely succeeded in my main, or subsidiary aims, I am fully aware, but the difficulties of the question will perhaps be accepted as a sufficient excuse.

In closing, I wish to acknowledge my indebtedness to those numerous editors and authors of works of recent date, to whom reference is made in the body of the essay, or in footnotes. I owe most to the admirable publications of the Hakluyt Society, without the aid of which, it is not too much to say, a work on such a subject as that of the present essay would demand the labour of years, rather than of months, and could be attempted by no one who was not a master of at least nine or ten entirely different languages.

The College, Llandovery, 1908.

CONTENTS

Contents

Travel & Travellers in India

CHAPTER I

Introduction

Ancient history is very much the history of the struggle for the transit trade of the East by the Persian Gulf and Red Sea.—*Sir George Birdwood.*

THE medieval period of Indian history may conveniently be regarded as opening with the first plundering expedition of Mahmud, "the Idol-Breaker," in 1001 A.D., and as reaching its close with the death of Aurangzib, in 1707 A.D. The chief documentary sources for the history of India during those seven centuries are the works of the various Mohammedan literary men—historians, annalists, scandal-retailers, gossipy memoir writers, poets, biographists, and autobiographists—who swarmed in the courts of the more enlightened of the rulers of Afghanistan, Hindustan, and the Deccan. Much of this mass of evidence, like the greater part of the history of Ferishta, and much of that of Khafi Khan, though immensely important, cannot lay claim to credence as being the work of a contemporary witness. A certain proportion of it, on the other hand, was written at or near the time of the events recorded, and sometimes, as, for instance, in the case of the royal autobiographists, possesses unique value and interest. The historian of India finds awaiting his researches such welcome mines of political and social observation as the personal memoirs of Tamerlane, or Baber, or Aurangzib, the accounts of their Indian experiences written by Arab or Persian travellers like Ibn Batuta and Abd-ur-Razzak, the contemporary evidence for Akbar's reign of writers like Nizam-ad-din and Abu-l-Fazl, and a number of other works by various Mohammedan courtiers or officials who were in a position to see what was taking place in their respective provinces or kingdoms, and possessed the ability to record it. The greater part of these sources for Indian history is available in an English form, being embodied in the valuable *History of India as told by its own Historians*, by the issue of which Sir H. M. Elliot and Professor Dowson placed all students of Indian history under an immense debt of gratitude. Valuable and, in the main, credible these native annalists undoubtedly are; but they have, as we might have expected, many serious defects. Like all Orientals they eulogise the reigning sovereign, exaggerating his good points and concealing his deficiencies.* They have

* An important exception to this generalisation is Abdul-Qadir Badaoni, a scholar and author of the time of Akbar. He was employed by that

little sense of history as an exact science. As a rule, they lack all sense of historical perspective, and we seldom meet a writer possessing the ability to reject information on true critical principles. From the point of view of the European reader, they leave still more to be desired. Being themselves Indians, and writing as they did for Indian readers, they not unnaturally assume in them familiarity with a number of local customs and institutions of which the ordinary European has no knowledge whatever. It is, therefore, peculiarly fortunate that for the last three hundred years of the medieval period of Indian history these native sources receive an immensely valuable supplement in the form of the accounts given by a host of Western travellers, of various nationalities, of their experiences in the East Indies. The following remark of Mr Stanley Lane-Poole, though originally made in reference to the travellers of the seventeenth century only, may fitly be applied to all: "In such a cloud of witnesses of varied ranks, professions, and nationalities, truth, divested of insular or continental prejudice, may surely be found. The body of information furnished by their journals, letters, and travels,

monarch in the work of making translations into Persian from Arabic and Sanskrit, and his remarks on his patron are frank and unreserved. Indeed, the chief merit of his *Muntakhab-ut-Tawarikh* is the fact that it is written by an enemy of Akbar, and exhibits the weakness as well as the grandeur of the character of the greatest of the Mogul emperors. See Blochmann's *Translation of the Ain i Akbari* vol. I, p. 104, note 2.

is indeed of priceless value to the historian of India."* In the fifteenth century the number of European visitors to India was few and their evidence scanty, both as regards value and amount; in the sixteenth the number was far larger, and their evidence proportionately more valuable, though the monopolising policy of the Portuguese, who, while by their discoveries stimulating the curiosity of Europe, strove to repress its power of satisfying it, tended to discourage Indian travel in all but their own countrymen. But in the seventeenth century, when it became evident that India was not to be for ever a private domain of Portugal, the tide set full and strong, and, one after another, men landed at Surat, or Goa, or some other convenient port, and set forth on their travels. In almost all who could lay claim to any literary skill,—and in not a few who could not,—India bred the "cacoëthes scribendi." They came, they saw, and, though conquest was reserved for a later era, at least they wrote. Their books vary in value from the political philosophy of a Bernier to the gossip of an Ovington, but there is not one of them who does not in some way increase our knowledge. It is the purpose of this essay to give an account of these travellers, and to try to estimate their importance as witnesses to the social institutions of the natives, and the nature and influence of Indian

* *Mediæval India under Mohammedan Rule*, p. 294.

Governments during the three centuries under review.

Before entering upon the account proper of the European travellers in India during these three centuries, it will be convenient, firstly, as defining the limits of the present work, to state the interpretation which has, for the purposes of this essay, been put upon the word "traveller"; and secondly, as tending to a clearer appreciation of the aims and knowledge with which the travellers visited India, in addition to conducing to a firmer grasp of the subject as a whole, to sketch the history of previous intercourse, both commercial and political, between Europe and India.

Every one of the few Europeans who went to India in the fifteenth century has an indisputable right to the name of traveller, and deserves mention as such in this work. It is obvious, however, that, when we come to the sixteenth and seventeenth centuries more discrimination is necessary. At first glance the choice of a criterion seems a simple matter; in reality it is very difficult. An account, for instance, of all the famous Portuguese who were in India in the sixteenth century would be interesting, and, in a certain sense, at any rate, relevant to the subject of the present work. Historians like Da Couto and Castanheda, professional men like Garcia da Orta, missionaries like St Francis Xavier, lawgivers like Menezes, a poet such as

Camoens, greatest of Portuguese poets, statesmen and warriors like

> Pacheco, foremost warrior of his age,
> Almeida, feared and mourned, the scourge of crimes,
> Stern Albuquerque, Castro strong and sage,
> And all with whom e'en Death a bootless strife must wage,*

were each and all of them real travellers; and yet any reference to these famous men cannot be more than incidental. It is the same with many of the leading Dutchmen, Frenchmen, and British in the following century. An account of all the well-known men who found careers in India during the two hundred years which followed Vasco da Gama's discovery, would practically transform the present work into a history of the growth of European influence in India. But it is not easy to say where the line must be drawn. The broad principle must, of course, be the existence of some record of the traveller's wanderings and observations. But such a record cannot be made absolutely a *sine qua non*. No account of Indian travel can omit the names of Covilham and Coryat; yet neither of them has left any description of what he saw in India. The principle of demarcation adopted in this work is, perhaps, somewhat unscientific; but a rough and ready criterion was the utmost that was possible under the circumstances. All professed travellers, such, for instance, as Coryat or de Montfart, will receive

* Camoens' *Lusiad*, I, xiv (Duff's Translation).

mention, whether the account which they wrote of their travels is worthless or has perished; those who were only travellers because their work required them to be so—and these are by far the greater number—will be included, if they left behind them a fair record of their observations, or a more ambitious work which was, in the main, based upon their Indian travels. These two principles enable us to include men like Covilham, of whose travels no record exists, and like Tavernier, whose travels were entirely subsidiary to his business; and while permitting the works of Bernier to receive attention, prevent us being compelled to give an account of da Couto, Castanheda, or da Orta, whose writings, though here and there they shed some light on the India of their day, can yet scarcely be said to be based mainly upon their travels. It is possible that the line of demarcation has on occasion been overstepped, but it will be found that doubtful claims to inclusion have generally been decided by the application of the principles given above.

It is of primary importance to remember that Vasco da Gama did not discover India in the sense in which Columbus may be said to have discovered America.* Both men sought a sea

* The sketch which now follows of the history of the intercourse between Europe and the "East Indies" prior to the opening of the fifteenth century is of necessity compressed and devoid of detail. For a fuller account the reader is referred to Dr William Robertson's *India* (Historical Works, vol. XI).

route to India; da Gama succeeded, Columbus failed. But neither discovered, nor could have discovered, India, which long before had been visited by Europeans, and did not need discovery. Its spices had long been modifying the history of Europe. The entire record of the intercourse between Europe and India from the very earliest times up to the present may, perhaps, be said to be the story of the struggle for the Indian trade. Sir George Birdwood in his valuable supplement to his *Report on the old Records of the India Office*, which he entitled *The Modern Quest and Invention of the Indies*, went so far as to say that "the history of modern Europe, and emphatically of England, is the history of the quest of the aromatic gum resins and balsams, and condiments and spices, of India, Further India, and the Indian Archipelago."* It was upon this view of the overwhelming importance of the Indian trade to the modern commercial world that Professor Stanley Jevons based his support of the much ridiculed theory of a connection between solar and commercial activity.† Sir George Birdwood's conclusion may be an overstatement of the case, or it may not; but at all events it is surely apparent, even to a mind devoid of all knowledge of the principles of

* p. 101 in the edition of 1891.

† See Prof. Jevons's letter in the *Times* of April 19, 1879, which is quoted at length on pp. 101–5 of Sir G. Birdwood's *Report on the Old Records*.

political economy, that in the middle ages, at least, and, indeed, in both the ante- and post-classical periods, a monopoly of, or predominant share in, the trade with the countries vaguely known as "India," comprising as they did a half, or more than a half, of the world's total population, must have been of the last importance to any commercial nation lucky or energetic enough to oust its rivals from it.

The earliest civilisation connected with Europe of which any traces exist is that which Mr Arthur Evans has shown to have existed on the shores of the Ægean Sea. 2500 B.C. may, perhaps, be assumed as the earliest date which can safely be accepted in connection with this. In the present state of our knowledge it would be too much to state dogmatically that there was no knowledge of nor intercourse with India at this date; but it seems very improbable, as in Homeric and classical times what little knowledge there was of India existing among the Greeks was rather suited to the mists of the poet than to the exactness of the historian or the geographer. All that Herodotus* can tell us is that India is the wealthiest and most populous country on earth, that Darius I conquered its western part, and that Indians served in the Persian army. Whether it was

* The "India" of Herodotus extends eastward no further than the countries bordering on what was considered to be the river of India, namely, the Indus.

India from which Solomon obtained gold, silver, apes, and peacocks, may be doubted; but, at all events, it is certain that his Phœnician allies at an earlier date than this carried on a vigorous trade between the Mediterranean coast of Asia and the shores of the Persian Gulf, and not improbably extended their enterprise as far as the mouths of the Indus and the Guzerat ports.

Real European knowledge of India began in 327 B.C. In that year Alexander stood on the right bank of the Beas, and, straining his eyes across the burning desert, which by its mere prospect had turned his soldiers' hearts to water, saw with the eyes of faith all India lying defenceless at his feet. But he was not destined to seize the prize which his marvellous exploits had put almost within his grasp. The enthusiasm of the leader had at last proved incapable of sustaining the enthusiasm of his men. India was destined to enjoy yet another thousand years of repose before a foreign invader was to shock her out of her age-long sleep. Sadly Alexander retraced his steps, and went back to Babylon to die. But this brief contact of Greece and India bore abundant fruit, and the Punjab of to-day still bears the impress of the great "Iskender."* After Alexander's departure

* Though Candahar is scarcely within the region of the five rivers, it is worth mentioning the fact that the name is merely a corruption of "Alexandria," and is the modern equivalent of "Alexandria in Arachosia." Grote, judging from the silence of Arrian, Curtius, and Diodorus, is

a vigorous overland trade sprang up between Europe and Asia, and continued with little interruption, by one route or another, until it was subverted by the discovery of a sea route round the Cape of Good Hope. The cities which Alexander founded on the Indus and its branches proved of the highest importance to the newly-established trade; while Nearchus's survey of the coasts from the Indus to the Tigris, and the subsequent embassies of Seleucus* and the Ptolemies† at the same time consolidated the trade and not only gave European geographers an increased knowledge of what is now Afghanistan and Baluchistan, but acquainted them with the plains of the lower Indus and the Ganges. The publication of the *Periplus of the Erythræan Sea*‡ conveyed the knowledge of the existence of the Guzerat and Malabar ports, as well as of Masulipatam on the Coromandel coast, and " the Gangetic Mart " at the head of the " great bay " of Bengal; while Ptolemy's " Tables " show that in 150 A.D. traders were acquainted with the ports on both sides of the Bay of Bengal, though

inclined to assert that the city was founded by one of Alexander's successors. See Grote's *History of Greece*, Part II, chap. xciv (edit. 1862, vol. VIII, p. 416, note 5).

* This was the famous embassy of Megasthenes, who was perhaps the first European to see the Ganges. The substance of his narrative, which is lost, has been transmitted by Diodorus Siculus, Strabo, and Arrian. Onesicritus, who accompanied him, wrote the earliest account which we possess of " Taprobane " or Ceylon.

† The Ptolemies established a route via the Red Sea and the Nile.

‡ Probably A.D. 200. C. Müller says A.D. 80–90.

their knowledge did not extend further east than Singapore.

Before this the power of the Phœnicians, which had survived the alleged (B.C. 586) and real (B.C. 332) destruction of Tyre, and the fall of Carthage (B.C. 146), had been broken at Actium in B.C. 31; but the Indian trade which this blow caused them largely to relinquish went on in other hands; and Rome, as mistress of Egypt, found herself able to reap much of the profit drawn from it. The *Periplus* which has been already mentioned, tells us that a certain Hippalus boldly set out from the mouth of the Arabian Gulf, and was carried by the south-western monsoon to Musiris,* a port of Malabar. The extent of the commerce which thus fell virtually beneath the control of Rome, even though her own merchants did not monopolise it, may be gauged in some measure from the remark of Pliny: "In no year does India drain our empire of less than five hundred and fifty millions of sesterces,† giving back her own wares in exchange, which are sold at fully one hundred times their prime cost." This passage, it may be remarked in passing, irresistibly recalls both Bernier's theory that India is the final destination of all the money in the world,‡ and the objections, based on false

* Mangalore.

† Coins of the reigns of Nero and Tiberius have been found buried in India.

‡ "It should not escape notice that gold and silver, after circulating in

economic theories, which were opposed in early days to the commercial enterprises of the English in the East Indies.

Ptolemy, the geographer, has a great deal of information on India in his work, and though he is less accurate as to details than the author of the *Periplus*, he yet exhibits a large amount of topographical knowledge. Mr Major not inaptly styles him the Hakluyt of his day.*

Intercourse now continued without interruption until the reign of Justinian, though there was but little accretion of actual knowledge. A slight decline was noticeable after the partition of the Roman Empire, though as long as the Eastern Empire survived it remained the centre of a vigorous commercial intercourse between East and West. Towards the close of the first half of the sixth century a merchant named Cosmas, who traded extensively in the Red Sea, wrote an account of the commerce between Egypt and India in his day, and gained for himself the title of "Indicopleustes." His evidence for the condition of the Indian trade is very clear, and gives the *Topographia Christiana*, which is still preserved, high rank in the literature of the subject.†

every other quarter of the globe, come at length to be absorbed in Hindostan." (Bernier, Irving Brock's Translation, p. 226, vol. 1.)

* *India in the Fifteenth Century* (Hakluyt Society Publication).

† It is worthy of remark that embassies of "Indians" to the Roman Emperor were not unknown, though the exact meaning of the word "Indians" is not always beyond dispute. Gibbon (chap. xviii) mentions

In the next century Persia and Egypt fell beneath the power of the Arabs, and one of the spoils of their victory was the Indian trade. The establishment of Busrah, between the junction of the Tigris and the Euphrates and the Persian Gulf, by the Khalif Omar settled it still more firmly in their hands, and from now onward the Arabs practically monopolised the Indian trade, all the carrying from India to the Levant being done by them, and Europeans being only allowed to help distribute the cargoes in Europe. Between Cosmas Indicopleustes and Marco Polo all the well-known travellers in India were Mohammedan.* Of Arab travellers there were many. In the ninth century an unknown adventurer visited the country of the "Maharajah,"† the Concan coast, Ceylon, and other places; with the result that the story of Sindbad the Sailor, which, though cast in fictitious shape, was based on some real Arab voyage of discovery in Indian waters, is valuable by no means solely as romance. We

Constantine as having received the congratulations of Æthiopians, Persians, and Indians. See Eusebius, in Vit. Const., IV, 50.

* Sighelmus of Sherborne (A.D. 883) is a possible, though improbable, exception. He is reputed to have visited the tomb of St Thomas at Maliapur. Gibbon, *Decline and Fall*, chap. xlvii, remarks "According to the legends of antiquity the gospel was preached in India by St Thomas. At the end of the ninth century, his shrine, perhaps in the neighbourhood of Madras, was devoutly visited by the ambassadors of Alfred, and their return with a cargo of pearls and spices rewarded the zeal of the English monarch." In a sceptical note, however, he adds "I almost suspect that the English ambassadors collected their cargo and legend in Egypt."

† It is doubtful whom this means. It is too early for the King of Vijayanagar, who bore the title later.

hear also of two Arab merchants who visited India and China in the ninth and tenth centuries. Suleiman and Abu Zaid, the two in question, were the first Western writers who made mention of tea and porcelain.* Ibn-Khurdadbah, another traveller, wrote toward the end of the ninth century. Masudi of Baghdad, Ibn Haukel, and Edrisi of Sicily, who flourished between the tenth and the twelfth centuries, enable us to realise the strength of the Arab grip upon the Indian trade. Arab merchants, we learn, had settled in considerable numbers in Guzerat, Cambay, and Malabar, and also had a certain though limited commerce with the country round the Jumna and the Ganges.

Shortly before the time of Masudi, the old trade route via Egypt, which had been superseded by the Arab route by Busrah, began to be reopened. This was due to the commercial energy of the city of Venice, whose great trade in Eastern spices, drugs, and silks dates from about the beginning of the ninth century. Alexandria and Constantinople were the chief cities through which the treasures of the East passed before reaching her ships. Genoa, which had traded in the Levant even before Venice, but had been prevented by that city from establishing commercial relations with Alexandria for a share in the Indian commerce

* Abbé Renaudot's *Anciennes Relations des Indes et de la Chine* (Paris, 1718).

which came by the Aden route, about the beginning of the fourteenth century opened a regular trade with Trebizond. An effective stimulus was administered by the Crusades, and the eyes of Europe being opened to the advantage to be gained from commerce with the East, Amalfi, Pisa, Florence, and other cities were not slow to demand their right to take part in it. Thus was founded that medieval network of trade routes between India and the Mediterranean upon which was based, to a large degree, the opulence and power of the City States of Italy. Three events, all occurring within the space of sixty years, subverted the prosperity of these cities, and ruined their trade with India. Constantinople fell before the advance of the Turk in A.D. 1453; in A.D. 1516–17 Selim annexed Syria and Egypt to the Ottoman Empire; after the first but before the second event Vasco da Gama doubled the Cape of Good Hope and discovered a sea route to India. Before the shock of the first blow Genoese prosperity fell in ruins, and that of Venice tottered; the second dealt the latter city a still severer stroke, and nothing but her wide commercial relations and her extraordinary vitality enabled her to continue with a renewed vigour which eventually rendered Famagusta instead of Alexandria the trading centre of the Levant; but when the full results of the third began to be felt, though in the actual event it was really only a coup-de-grâce to the already dying Venetian commerce, it became abundantly clear that, even had Italian commercial prosperity been at its height, it could not have been maintained in competition with the discoverers of a sea route to India.

A natural outcome of the course which the history of the Levant followed during the centuries which elapsed between the Crusades and Vasco da Gama's discovery was the rivalry of Christian and Mohammedan for the profits of the Indian trade. It is, therefore, peculiarly appropriate that of the two most famous travellers during that period the Venetians gave us one, the Arabs the other. Marco Polo started from Venice on his travels in 1271; Ibn Batuta left Tangiers in 1325. It is unfortunate that both these famous travellers lie outside the direct scope of this work; but no account of the travellers even of a later date can afford to pass them by in silence. Marco Polo's remarkable book was the direct inspiration of the travelling enterprise of two and three hundred years later. The visionary edifices which the imagination of the early discoverers reared were often fantastic, and must to their soberer contemporaries have often seemed like unsubstantial castles in the air; but their foundations were laid, solid and deep, in the pages of Marco Polo's book. His work is valuable as a picture of the commercial state and artistic development of India and the East; "in brief," says Sir George Birdwood, it is "one of those like the Bible, the *Iliad* and *Odyssey*, the *History of Herodotus* and *Pliny's Natural History*, 'that shew, contain, and nourish all the world';* books we never tire of, for they are always fresh."† Medieval Europe heard with astonishment of the worship of the cow;‡ it marvelled to read of the people's abstention from animal food, and their voluntary self-immolation in honour of their god§; it gasped as it pictured to itself the spectacle of devoted wives casting themselves on the funeral pyre by their dead husband's side.‖ Slowly but steadily the contents of the book became known, and wherever it went it stimulated an immense curiosity to see what Marco Polo had seen, and to share in the wealth which he had described. It is safe to say that had Marco Polo never travelled, or never given his experiences to the world, the momentous discoveries of Columbus, Magellan, and Gama, as well as the heroic though fruitless endeavours after the North-West Passage, would, for want of the stimulus to the imagination so necessary in such enterprises, have been postponed for several generations.

* *Love's Labour's Lost*, Act IV, scene 3.

† Supplementary Note to the *Report on the Old Records of the India Office*, p. 125.

‡ *The Book of Ser Marco Polo* (Yule's Translation, edited by Cordier, 1903), ii, 341. § ii, 340, 341. ‖ ii, 341.

Ibn Batuta's travels are likewise of immense interest and importance, but they have, for some reason or other, not attracted a tithe of the attention which Marco Polo's book obtained. His travels, which began in 1325, lasted twenty-four years; by the end of 1334 he had visited Alexandria (travelling across Africa from Tangiers), Palestine, Syria, Arabia, Quiloa (south of Zanzibar on the East coast of Africa), Ormuz, Mecca, Asia Minor, Theodosia (on the Black Sea), part of lower Russia, Constantinople, Khorasan, Cabul, and Delhi. At Delhi he stayed eight years, till in 1342 he was sent by Mohammed Taghlak on an embassy to China. On his way thither he visited Calicut, Honawar, Ceylon, the Maldives, Bengal and Sumatra. On returning from China, he travelled home by way of Baghdad, Damascus and Jerusalem to Fez, which he reached in 1349. Ibn Batuta is fully entitled to a place among the great Asiatic travellers, and it is astonishing that he has not attracted more attention. His account is valuable, apart from the information it contains on the condition of India under Mohammed Taghlak, as exhibiting the wide extent of the Arab commercial intercourse with the East prior to its partial demolition by the growth of the Ottoman power, and its final destruction by the Portuguese discovery of a sea route to India.

The remaining travellers who helped still further to initiate the Western world into the mysteries of India in the times anterior to the opening of the fifteenth century may be briefly mentioned. Marino Sanuto, a nobleman of Venice, travelled in the East* in 1300–1306, and in his book† gives some valuable evidence as to the route of the Venetian commerce with India at that time. Ten years after Sanuto's return the famous Minorite Friar Odorico di Pordenone set out for Ormuz, whence he went by land to "Tana," in Salsette, near what is now Bombay, to gather the bones of four missionaries who had been murdered there in 1321, and buried by Friar Jordanus, a missionary traveller who visited India at that date.‡ From this place he went on by sea to "Polumbum" (Quilon), "Sillan" (Ceylon), the Coromandel Coast, China, and a number of other places. John de Marignolli, a Minorite Friar likewise, after going overland to Pekin in a missionary capacity, touched India on his return home in 1347. Among other places visited by him in India was the shrine of St Thomas on the Coromandel Coast, always a spot of the greatest interest to the early Christian visitors to India. Finally we may mention Sir John Mandeville, who, however, in spite of his wonderful narrative,§ which

* Apparently not in India.

†"Liber secretorum fidelium Crucis super Terræ Sanctæ recuperatione."

‡ Jordanus wrote a short quaint account of his travels, which has been translated and issued as one of the Hakluyt Society's Publications.

§ Published in 1499, it is sometimes erroneously said to have been the first English book to appear in print. The *Recuyell of the Historyes of Troye* was much earlier (1474).

seems to show that he travelled throughout the countries of the East between 1327 and 1372, has no claim to inclusion among Indian travellers. "He speaks," says Sir George Birdwood, acutely enough, "of 'the marvyles of Inde,' but it is certain he was never there. He may be described as the father of English sensation writers, and is not to be trusted even when he may be telling the truth."* Further mention may be safely denied him.

As has been shown, the list of early-medieval visitors from Europe and the Mediterranean coasts to India is no mean one. And yet the fifteenth and sixteenth century travellers went to India with practically a blank mind, and quite unprepared for what they saw. The explanation is to be found in the slow and small circulation of books in the Middle Ages. A traveller might write a book describing what he had seen in the East, but its contents reached an extremely limited class even among educated men. In 1400 A.D. the man of average knowledge knew little more of India than he had known in 1000 A.D., probably less than he had known in 100 or 500 A.D., when the *Periplus* or *Topographia Christiana* had caused a certain knowledge of India and the East in general to spread downwards from the circles of the bookish into the popular mind. We are fortunate in that we are in a position to gauge the extent of the

* *Report on the Old Records*, etc., p. 133.

knowledge of India possessed by an average man of affairs at the opening of the fifteenth century. In 1403 A.D. Ruy Gonzalez de Clavijo was sent on an embassy by the King of Portugal to the court of Tamerlane at Samarcand. He did not go to India; but Timur had not long before made his devastating descent upon North India, and Clavijo gathered a certain amount of information about the country at Timur's capital. This hearsay evidence he inserted in the highly interesting account of his embassy which he wrote on his return.* What the writer says of India is not a little diverting, and at the same time clearly exhibits the absolute lack of knowledge of the country which he assumes in his readers. A short quotation may be illustrative:

"The chief city of India is called Delhi. . . . They say that there are many great towns and cities, and that the country is very rich and populous.† . . . The people and the lord of India are Christians of the Greek faith, but among them there are some who are distinguished by a brand in their faces, and who are despised by the others, and Moors and Jews live among them, but they are subject to the Christians.‡. . . The Emperor of Cathay used to be a Gentile, but he was converted to the faith of the Christians."§

* *Narrative of the Embassy of Ruy Gonzalez de Clavijo to the Court of Timour, at Samarcand,* A.D. 1403–1406. *Translated for the first time . . . by C. R. Markham, F.R.G.S.* (Hakluyt Society Publication, 1859.)

† Clavijo need not have gone to Samarcand to learn this. Herodotus uses practically the same language. ‡ p. 153. § p. 174.

Such was the extraordinary combination of fact, platitude, and absurdity, with which a writer could without fear of ridicule regale his fellow ignorants in Europe. But the hour was fast approaching when the first of that long line of modern travellers, the first of that long line of men who in modern times have deliberately balanced the chances of death on the one hand with those of profit and adventure on the other, was to set foot on the soil of India, and on his return was to commence the task, which so many of his successors have helped to further, of making India better known to Europe. Once well started, the stream of men became well nigh unceasing. The silent Siren voice called across the lands and seas to the adventurous spirits of Europe, and they hearkened and gladly obeyed. For one who returned safely a thousand were inflamed to go. The combination of novelty, excitement, adventure, and gain proved an overwhelming attraction that captivated the imaginations of all save those whose spiritual fibre was utterly devoid of elasticity. Eagerly men embraced any opportunity of visiting the "East Indies" that presented itself. Dangers and discomforts, by sea and land, were ignored; shipwreck, heat, robbery, murder, disease, treachery, they recked not of; the more brightly coloured parts of the picture so dazzled them that they could not see the darker; and so they hastened, some by land and some by sea, to satisfy by a single act a wide assortment of various desires. Here, as everywhere, realisation sometimes belied anticipation; now and then a traveller, sick for home, and weary of strange surroundings, harboured those thoughts which a gifted Anglo-Indian poet* put so well hundreds of years later:—

> He did list to the voice of a siren,
> He was caught by the clinking of gold;
> And the slow toil of Europe seemed tiring,
> And the gray of his fatherland cold.
> He must haste to the gardens of Circe;
> What ails him, the slave, that he frets
> In thy service? O Lady, sans merci!
> O land of Regrets!

On the whole, however, delight and astonishment, not to speak of "the clinking of gold," drove away from these early travellers all other thoughts, and saved them from that melancholy and pessimism which has pervaded much of that English literature which has since their day grown up in India, and is so well exemplified in the poem from which the above extract is taken. Most of their records are simple and straightforward accounts of what they saw and heard in India. A few use their experiences as texts, Parson Terry,† for instance, for his delightful sermons, Bernier for his economic and political

* Sir Alfred Lyall, in *Verses written in India.*

† The "weighing" of the Great Mogul, for instance, which will be mentioned later, enabled the Rev. Edward Terry to adduce the Biblical parallel of Beltashazzar, who was weighed in the balance and found wanting. Daniel v, 27; Terry's *Voyage to East India*, ed. of 1655, p. 396.

discourses. But almost all of them are honest unsophisticated witnesses, a little credulous, perhaps, but comparing well in this respect with travellers generally, who are a gullible race, and always, almost without exception, seeking to discover the real truth. The consequence is that these travellers' narratives not only form the most delightful and entertaining reading, but are, from some points of view, absolutely unique among the documentary sources for the history of any country.

CHAPTER II

Three Fifteenth-Century Pioneers

The Tibr when from its native mine cast forth
Appears as vile unprofitable earth;
  The aloes wood enjoys but slight esteem
In its own land,—mere fuel for the hearth;
Let either quit the country of its birth,
  The one an ore all-coveted we deem,
The other a perfume of priceless worth.

—*Arabian Epigram.**

IN 1400 A.D. there was no one kingdom in India overwhelmingly superior in power to the rest. Ala-ad-Din Khilji, the famous King of Delhi, had, at the beginning of the preceding century, carried his arms from the Punjab in the north to Cape Comorin in the south, and gained a truer right to call himself Emperor of India than any Oriental ruler, before or since, has ever possessed. His magnificent empire had, ever since his death in 1316 A.D., been in process of decay. The ruin had been begun by the mad schemes of Mohammed Taghlak (1325–1351 A.D.), had been accelerated by the futile gentleness of Firoz (1351–1388 A.D.), and was finally consummated in 1398 A.D. by Timur's fearful and devastating visitation. Henceforward, until

* Verified by the Rev. P. G. Hill, and printed in the edition of Ludovico di Varthema's travels which has been published by the Hakluyt Society

the reign of Akbar, the history of India can scarcely be said to centre round one main kingdom. The capital from which India had been governed became the centre of an insignificant sovereignty. The Seiads (1414–1450) and the Lodis (1450–1526) of Delhi are dismissed by Elphinstone in but five pages of his six-hundred page history of Hindu and Mohammedan India.* From the days of Timur to those of his great descendant Akbar, India was a congeries of small and often mutually antagonistic kingdoms. The Bahmani kingdom of the Deccan had established itself at Culbarga in 1347. Even before this the great Hindu principality of Vijayanagar had formed itself into the bulwark of Southern India against further Mohammedan aggression. Bengal threw off the yoke in 1338. The "Kings of the East" became independent at Jaunpur in 1394. Guzerat rebelled in 1396. Candesh followed suit three years later. Malwa broke away in 1401. In Multan and in Bikanir, at Biana, Kampila, Patiala, and many other places within easy reach of Delhi, various princes did not hesitate to defy the fallen monarchs. Hindu rajahs, whose submission had at best been little more than nominal, automatically refused tribute; others like those of Orissa, who had never bowed the knee, breathed more freely. In Sind and the Punjab in the north, on the Malabar and Coro-

* Elphinstone's *History of India*, edition of 1849, pp. 363–367. In Cowell's (ninth) edition, 1905, pp. 408–413.

mandel coasts in the south, various chiefs, more or less powerful, exercised independent sway. While India remained in this distracted condition she had no history. The annals of these kingdoms, says Mr Lane-Poole, are "either unwritten or unworthy of record." This was the uninspiring state of affairs in India at the opening of the fifteenth century, and it remained unchanged in all but minor details till the dissolution of the Bahmani empire, the coming of the Portuguese, and, a little later, the invasion of Baber, profoundly modified the situation, and paved the way for a drastic rearrangement of political power.

How many Europeans actually set foot in India during the fifteenth century it is impossible to say with absolute certainty. Accounts are extant of the experiences of three travellers; that of a fourth has perished.* The three, whose accounts, written either by themselves or others, we possess, are Nicolo de'Conti, a Venetian, Athanasius Nikitin, a Russian, and Hieronimo di Santo Stefano, a Genoese. From the mere chance which gave us the narrative of Conti, and the long disappearance of the manuscript of Nikitin, we may perhaps safely assume that there were several others, whose very names have been forgotten.

* This fourth traveller was Pedro Covilham. He was earlier than Stefano, but further mention of him is postponed to the next chapter, where it will be more in place.

Three Fifteenth-Century Pioneers

By far the earliest and most important of these was Nicolo de'Conti. Sprung from a noble Venetian house, he was early initiated at Damascus into the mysteries of that commerce which was the basis of Venetian prosperity. In 1419, accompanied by his wife, he set out from Damascus upon his twenty-five years' travel in the East. Having joined a caravan of six hundred other merchants, he passed over the deserts of Arabia Petraea and through Chaldaea to "Baldochia" (Baghdad), whence he sailed down the Euphrates to Busrah. Reaching Ormuz he went to Kalhat in Arabia, where he stayed a considerable time in order to learn Persian, his knowledge of which subsequently stood him in no little stead. The first India town at which he touched was the flourishing port of Cambay, in which he chiefly remarked the abundance of sardonyxes and suttees. Continuing his voyage along the coast, after twenty days' sailing he arrived at two cities on the seashore, "one named Pacamuria, and the other Helly." Disembarking, apparently at one of these places, he ventured three hundred miles inland, inspired by a desire to behold the splendours of the far-famed capital of the kingdom of "Bizenegalia."* Of this city he gives a very fair

*** This is Vijayanagar. Later travellers adopt various methods of spelling the word, e.g., Bisnaga, Bicheneger, Bidjanagar. The worst barbarity, however, in this line is Beejanuggur, which of itself is sufficient to justify the extremest advocates of orthographic reform in connection with Indian names.**

account. Eight days from Vijayanagar brought him to "Pelagonda" (? Paliconda, now Ongule), a "very noble city," and twenty more to the seaport of "Peudifetania,"* whence he seems to have gone to Maliapur, the Mecca of the Nestorian Christians, and the reputed burial place of St Thomas. His further wanderings, in which we need not follow him in detail till his return to India proper, took him to Ceylon, which he asserts is three thousand miles round, Sumatra, to which he is the first to apply the erroneous identification with the "Taprobana" of antiquity, and "Ternassari,"† to which place he had a stormy sea passage from Sumatra. Proceeding thence to the mouth of the Ganges, he sailed up the river till he came to "Cernove."‡ Continuing his journey up the river, Conti finally reached the "very powerful city of Maarazia."§ He then returned to "Cernove," and after visiting "Buffetania" (Burdhwan), turned eastward again, and went to Arracan, the Irrawaddy, Ava, Pegu, Java, and Sumbawa, where he stayed nine months. On his return to Cambay by sea, he touched at "Coloen" (Quilon), in Travancore, "Cocym" (Cochin), and Calicut, in addition to a number

* Duma-Patnam, near Tellicherry (R. H. Major). Pudipatana, on the Malabar Coast (Sir George Birdwood).

† Probably Tennasserim. It is not clear, however, that "Ternasseri" is not some other (unidentified) place.

‡ Mr Major (*India in the Fifteenth Century*, Hak. Soc.) suggests that "Cernove" is Karunagar.

§ Mr Major suggests that this is Mathura.

of other places. At Calicut he noticed, like almost all subsequent visitors to that place, the flagrant polyandry of certain classes of the people, the conventions relating thereto, and the extraordinary laws of inheritance which were necessitated by such unusual marriage customs. From Cambay he returned home by the ordinary trade route through Egypt, but at Carrae, by a cruel piece of irony on the part of Fate, he had the misfortune, when almost within sight of home, to lose his wife and two of the children who had shared his dangers. Conti reached his native city in 1444. The story of the circumstance which led to a narrative of his travels being given to the world is curious. During his travels Conti had once, while in Egypt, been compelled to abjure his religion in order to save his wife and his children from death. Some five years after his return, troubled in conscience by the memory of his faithlessness, Conti sought absolution from Pope Eugene the Fourth for his sin. The Pope was exceedingly happy in his choice of a penance for the erring wanderer. He ordered him to relate his adventures to Poggio Bracchiolini, his famous secretary, who wrote a Latin version of them which appeared in the fourth book of his treatise, *De Varietate Fortunae*,* and constitutes one of the best books of early travel which we possess. The shrewd and careful observations

* Edited by the Abbé Oliva, Paris, 1723.

of Conti are given us in the words of a scholar and a cultured man, a combination which does not reappear in the history of Indian travel for many years. His evidence for Vijayanagar, to pass over the rest of his observations, is of the highest value, and will be referred to again before the close of the present chapter.

A quarter of a century had elapsed since Conti's departure when the Russian, Athanasius Nikitin, set forth upon a commercial visit to India. In 1468 he left his native place Tver, and travelled down the Volga to the Caspian Sea. After being robbed at Astrakan, and subsequently imprisoned, he pushed on to Baku, where, as he graphically puts it, "the fire burns unextinguished,"* and to Bokhara, at that time a great centre of Eastern commerce. Retracing his steps, Nikitin stayed for some time at Sari in Mazanderan, after which he traversed the north and west provinces of Persia until he reached Ormuz. Here he took ship and crossed the "Doria Hondustankaia" (the Indian Ocean), to Muscat, Guzerat, Cambay, and Chaul, at which last place he disembarked. From Chaul he turned his steps inland past Junair to Bidar, which he calls "Beuruk." At Bidar Nikitin stayed four years. The details of his observations at this place which he gives in his account are of the highest importance, as Bidar had, not

* The naphtha springs and mud volcanoes of Abscharon are the "fires" referred to.

many years before his arrival, been made the capital of the Bahmani sovereignty in preference to Culbarga, the former capital. Culbarga, as well as " Pervota " (Parwattam), " the Jerusalem of the Hindus,"* was also included in the scope of his visits. Nikitin's narrative also contains some very useful second-hand evidence as to Vijayanagar, for which the historian is by no means ungrateful; but it is to be regretted that he did not actually visit the city, and so cause his evidence to possess greater weight. At the end of his stay Nikitin returned to the Concan coast, and, embarking at Dabul for Ormuz, completed his return to Russia by overland, travelling via Shiraz, Ispahan, and Tabriz to Trebizond, and by a sea voyage from that port to Theodosia.† Whether he ever actually reached Tver is doubtful; there seems some evidence to show that he died before he reached Smolensk, and that his account of his travels, written by himself, was brought in 1475 by some merchants to Moscow. It is, under these circumstances, very fortunate that his narrative was not entirely lost or destroyed. It is a curious but highly interesting and valuable document. Nikitin was not a cultivated or philosophic observer; neither does he compensate for his lack of a comprehensive grasp of the political

* Nikitin's own phrase (*India in the Fifteenth Century*, iii, 16).

† Now Feodosia, on the bay of Kaffa, at the south-east of the Crimean Peninsula.

conditions around him by an accuracy or minuteness of detail. His narrative, too, is frequently obscured by long rhapsodies in Turkish, which even Turkish scholars find a difficulty in interpreting. But we could ill afford to dispense with him. His evidence for the Mohammedan sovereignty at Bidar in 1470, though not on a par with that of Conti for the Hindu kingdom of Vijayanagar some forty years earlier, has a certain definite value, while his remarks on Culbarga, as well as his second-hand information on Vijayanagar, are not to be despised.

Six years from the close of the century came the last of these three merchant adventurers, Hieronimo di Santo Stefano. The Genoese travelled from Cairo down the Nile to Keneh, and thence made his way across the desert to Kosseir on the Red Sea. He then sailed via Massowa to Aden, whence he crossed the Indian Ocean to the flourishing port of Calicut. Twenty-six days out of Calicut took him to Ceylon, and another twelve to an unidentified port on the Coromandel Coast. After visiting Pegu (where he lost his companion Adorno), Ava, Sumatra, and other places, he finally started for home. Having been detained six months by weather among the Maldives, he subsequently suffered shipwreck, and reached Cambay in a state of absolute destitution. At Cambay a merchant took him into his service, and in the end he managed to go as supercargo to Ormuz, from which port he was able to travel to Tripoli through Persia. At Tripoli the unfortunate Genoese merchant's calamitous journey came to an end, and he stayed there to write the narrative of his woes. It possesses but little value from the point of view of the present work, for in addition to the fact that the traveller saw nothing of India beyond its coasts, his account is little more than a bare chronicle, and tells us little that we do not know from other sources.

Such were the travels of these three pioneers of the modern European exploitation of the commercial possibilities of India. It remains to be seen what light they shed upon the somewhat jejune Mohammedan records of fifteenth century India. Hieronimo di Santo Stefano may be ruled out at once as being practically valueless, and attention safely confined to what Conti and Nikitin tell us. It may be said at once that the evidence of these two men for the political condition of India is of far less value than that for its social institutions. When the Mohammedan writers leave us in the lurch as to a dynasty, a battle, or a date, Conti and Nikitin do not help us to fill the gap in our knowledge.

It is doubtful whether at the time of Conti's visit there was, with the possible exception of the Bahmani empire, a single kingdom, Hindu or Mohammedan, which was more powerful than the kingdom of which Vijayanagar was the capital city. The history of this kingdom, which till recently was but little known, and is still somewhat obscure in many points, has been admirably synthetised by Mr Sewell from the very scanty material which was all that was available for his patient researches.* Two sources upon which he draws considerably are the narratives of Conti and Nikitin. Conti tells us that the circumference of the city of Vijayanagar was sixty miles, and that the number of people living within it capable of bearing arms was ninety thousand. This was in the early days of the century, long before the kingdom had reached its acme of power under Krishna Deva Raya. Founded in 1336 it had continued to grow, and till 1565 remained the bulwark of Hindu independence against the encroachments of the Mohammedan kings of the Deccan, who, toward the close of the fifteenth century, carved for themselves independent kingdoms out of the ruins of the Bahmani dynasty. Before the downfall of the Bahmanis, Vijayanagar successfully, though with some trouble, and at the cost of constant defeats and a frequent payment of large tribute, prevented the Mohammedans from obtaining a firm footing beyond the Tungabudra and the Krishna. From Nikitin we have some sidelights on the almost unceasing war which was carried on by the Hindus and Mohammedans on the banks of

* *A Forgotten Empire* (*Vijayanagar*). A Contribution to the History of India. By Robert Sewell, M.R.A.S., F.R.G.S., London, 1900.

these rivers. Of Junair he says: "Here resides Asat, Khan of Indian Jooneer, a tributary of Meliktuchar. . . .* He has been fighting the Kofars for twenty years, being sometimes beaten, but mostly beating them." As to the extent of the kingdom Conti and Nikitin give us but little information; but we may perhaps be pardoned if we digress a moment to mention the evidence on this point of Abd-er-Razzak, a famous Arab traveller, who was in 1442 sent by the Shah of Persia on an embassy to the King of Vijayanagar—a significant fact, in itself conclusive evidence of the growing importance of the Hindu kingdom. From him we learn that the King of Vijayanagar was practically supreme from the Krishna river to Cape Comorin, and that even powerful ports like Calicut were not able to ignore him. "Although," he says, "the Samerit† is not subject to the laws of the King of Bidjanagar, he nevertheless pays him respect and stands extremely in fear of him, since, if what is said is true, this latter prince has in his dominions three hundred ports, each of which is equal to Calicut, and on *terra firma* his territories comprise a space of three months'

* By Meliktuchar Nikitin means Mahmud Gawan, a noble who was powerful under the reigns of Nizam Shah Bahmani, king of the Deccan (1461–1463), and his successor Mohammed II (1463–1482). During the reign of the latter Mahmud Gawan's enemies contrived an infamous forgery, and caused him to be put to death. This event happened in 1481, when the unfortunate victim was in the seventy-eighth year of his age. See Beale and Keene's *Oriental Biographical Dictionary*, ed. of 1894, p. 231.

† The Samorin, or King of Calicut.

journey."* To the greatness, power, and magnificence of the city all testify alike. Abd-er-Razzak employs the most extravagant hyperbole: "The city of Bidjanagar is such that the pupil of the eye has never seen a place like it, and the ear of intelligence has never been informed that there existed anything to equal it in the world." This, it should be remembered, is the testimony of a cultivated Persian ambassador, not a mere gaping ignoramus in search of sensation. Abd-er-Razzak estimated the King's army at 1,100,000 men; Nikitin's figures for the city alone are 100,000 foot and 50,000 horse. Conti does not mention the army in particular, which was probably less large at his earlier date, though he says of Indian armies generally: "Their armies consist of a million men and upwards"; but an idea of the general magnificence of the scale of the King's court may be gathered from the fact that he credits him with the possession of 12,000 wives. His picture of the uxorious monarch going forth with his feminine horde is, to say the least, diverting, and deserves quotation: "The inhabitants of this region marry as many wives as they please, who are burnt with their dead husbands. Their King is more powerful than all the other Kings of India. He takes to himself 12,000 wives, of whom 4,000 follow him on foot wherever he may go, and are employed solely in the service

* *India in the Fifteenth Century* (Hak. Soc.)

of the kitchen. A like number, more handsomely equipped, ride on horseback. The remainder are carried by men in litters, of whom 2,000 or 3,000 are selected as his wives on condition that at his death they should voluntarily burn themselves with him, which is considered to be a great honour for them."

The nature of the inter-racial wars between Vijayanagar and the Bahmani kingdoms can be clearly gathered from the narratives of Nikitin and Conti. Ballistae and "bombardas," says Conti, are used for besieging cities. Nikitin tells us, erroneously, that Vijayanagar was captured by Melikh Khan Khoda; but there is no need to doubt that his statement refers to the destruction of some city or other, and his allegation that the inhabitants, men and women alike, were beheaded to the number of twenty thousand, and that the rest, to the number of an additional twenty thousand, were sold into slavery, is significant of the internecine nature of these combats.

The strength of Vijayanagar consisted chiefly in its magnificent situation, which rendered it almost impregnable. Nikitin has a fine pen-picture of its position which makes it difficult to believe that he never saw the town. It is one of the few occasions on which he consents to be graphic: "The Hindu Sultan Kadam is a very powerful prince. He possesses a numerous army, and resides on a mountain at Bichenegher. This vast city is surrounded by three forts, and intersected by a river, bordering on one side on a dreadful jungle, and on the other on a dale, a wonderful place, and to any purpose convenient. On one side it is quite inaccessible; a road gives right through the town, and as the mountain rises high with a ravine below, the town is impregnable."

The only other Indian kingdom for the history of which the observations of any fifteenth century traveller are important is the kingdom of the Bahmanis. Nikitin is the only European whom we know to have visited Bidar in the fifteenth century, and even his remarks on what he saw there are somewhat more attenuated than could have been desired.

Nikitin describes Bidar as the chief city of Mohammedan India, and at the time the statement was probably true. He gives a highly-coloured description of the opulence of the court, and contrasts it with the misery of the country population: "The land is overstocked with people, but those in the country are very miserable, whilst the nobles are very opulent and delight in luxury. They are wont to be carried on their silver beds, preceded by some twenty chargers caparisoned in gold, and followed by three hundred men on horseback, and five hundred on foot, and by horn-men, ten torch-bearers, and ten musicians." The army with which the Sultan of Bidar marched against Vijayanagar consisted, according to Nikitin, of

900,000 men, 150,000 horse, and 575 elephants. The Sultan himself is described as being a little man, only twenty years of age, and completely dominated by his ambitious nobles, a circumstance almost too common in Indian history to deserve remark.

It is to be regretted that Conti does not tell us more of what he saw in Bengal, of which province at this date (1420) we know but little. His finding the banks of the Ganges, however, covered with towns, amidst beautiful gardens and orchards, and his passing four famous cities before he reached the opulent "Maarazia," is valuable as a tribute to the prosperous condition of the country. If to these remarks on Vijayanagar, the Bahmani capital, and Bengal, we add a few scattered notices of the political state of Cambay and of a few isolated places on the Malabar and Coromandel coasts, we have completed the list of places on the nature and influence of whose government the fifteenth century travellers shed any light. It is time to see what they tell us of their institutions.

In a burst of pessimism Nikitin said of the people of Bidar: "All are black and wicked, and the women all harlots, or witches, or thieves, or cheats; and they destroy their masters with poison."* It is perhaps due to his poor view of

* This disparagement of the people's "blackness" is paralleled in an amusing passage in Abd-er-Razzak's narrative, which is worth quoting: "As soon as I landed at Calicut I saw beings such as my imagination had never depicted the like of. Extraordinary beings, who are neither men nor

the character of the Indians that Nikitin, beyond saying that there are convenient inns for travellers, where " the food is cooked . . . . by the landlady," and that the people worship " Boot," and are separated by caste, and making a few other similar observations, does not condescend to describe to us the customs and institutions of the natives. For this information we must have recourse to Conti, who is very full and valuable. The only drawback to his information is that it is not always easy to know to which locality he wishes his remarks to apply.

It is interesting to learn from Conti of the existence and circulation of what was practically paper-money. He says that, in addition to the ordinary coinage, iron, Venetian ducats, and cards inscribed with the name of the king were accepted.

Conti has some exceedingly interesting evidence for the legal procedure of the time. His remarks seem to apply principally to Vijayanagar, but also, generally speaking, to all Hindu India which he visited. " The debtor who is insolvent," he says, " is everywhere adjudged to be the property of his creditor." In criminal law trial by ordeal held sway. He describes three methods, which are so extraordinarily foolish, that did we not remember that, at the

devils, at sight of whom the mind takes alarm; If I were to see such in my dreams my heart would be in a tremble for many years. I have had love passages with a beauty, whose face was like the moon; but I could never fall in love with a negress." See *India in the Fifteenth Century*, p. 16.

same time as Conti was in India, Europe was committing almost equal absurdities, we should be inclined to disbelieve him. If a man were accused of an offence, and no witness were produced to prove it, instead of adopting the sensible course, and putting the false accuser in some Indian equivalent for a pillory, the judge compelled the accused to swear before the idol that he was innocent, and then ordered him to lick a red-hot mattock with his tongue. If he were innocent, he was expected to feel only a pleasant sensation of warmth; but woe betide him if his tongue exhibited any sign of the contact! Carrying a red-hot plate in the hand, and immersing the fingers in boiling butter, were minor variants of this brilliant specimen of legal sagacity.

The rite of suttee seems to have been almost universal in Hindu India when Conti visited it, when the restraining influence of the Mohammedans had not as yet been greatly exerted. Such an amazing illustration of the truth of the principle embodied in the famous line of Lucretius* naturally riveted the attention of almost every European visitor to India. As, however, Conti's description is one of the best that we have from the pen of any early traveller, it is worth while to quote it *in extenso*, to avoid the necessity of any detailed account of the rite in reference to any other traveller who came in

* Tantum relligio potuit suadere malorum. Lucr. 1, 101.

contact with it. "In central India,"* he says, "the dead are burned, and the living wives, for the most part, are consumed in the same funeral pyre with their husband, one or more, according to the agreement at the time the marriage was contracted. The first wife was compelled by the law to be burnt, even though she should be the only wife. But others are married under the express agreement that they should add to the splendour of the funeral ceremony by their death, and this is considered a great honour for them. The deceased husband is laid on a couch, dressed in his best garments. A vast funeral pyre is erected over him in the form of a pyramid, constructed of odoriferous woods. The pile being ignited, the wife, habited in her richest garments, walks gaily round it, singing, accompanied by a great concourse of people, and amid the sounds of trumpets, flutes, and songs. In the meantime, one of the priests, called Bachali, standing on some elevated spot, exhorts her to a contempt of life and death, promising her all kinds of enjoyment with her husband, much wealth, and abundance of ornaments. When she has walked round the fire several times, she stands near the elevation on which is the priest, and taking off her dress, puts on a white linen garment, her body having first been washed according to custom. In

* By "central" India Conti means most of India proper. Further India is with him what is now Burma, nearer India is Persia and the north-west of India.

obedience to the exhortation of the priest, she then springs into the fire. If some show more timidity (for it frequently happens that they become stupefied by terror at the sight of the struggles of the others, or of their sufferings in the fire), they are thrown into the fire by the by-standers, whether consenting or not. Their ashes are afterwards collected and placed in urns, which form an ornament for the sepulchre." This graphic description of suttee, as it obtained in the fifteenth century, enables us to see quite clearly what this diabolical if heroic convention meant to the Hindu wife, and of the part played in it by a fiendish priesthood, which while claiming to be the oracle of God, has in India, as elsewhere, too often done the devil's work. In almost all the accounts we hear of suttee, the writer emphasises the part played by the Brahmin priests in stimulating the ebbing fanaticism of the unhappy devotees, even proceeding to such lengths as pushing the shrinking victim into the fiery pit. Other examples of their baleful influence are given by Conti in the instance he adduces of the self-immolation which they directly encouraged. We hear of an idol which was carried through the city of Vijayanagar, before which, as travellers tell us was done at Jaggernat, fanatics cast themselves to win a glorious martyrdom. Others made an incision in their side, inserted a rope through their body, and hung on as an ornament.* But most extraordinary of all is the account which Conti gives of a certain method of self-execution which was practised in the great Hindu capital. It well deserves quotation. Many present themselves "having on their neck a broad circular piece of iron, the fore part of which is round, and the hinder part exceedingly sharp. A chain attached to the fore part hangs suspended on the breast, into which the victims, sitting down with their legs drawn up and their neck bent, insert their feet. Then on the speaker pronouncing certain words, they suddenly stretch out their legs, and at the same time drawing up their neck, cut off their own head, yielding up their lives as a sacrifice to their idols."

In addition to what has been already given, Conti's book contains a considerable amount of other useful information. He gives a fair account of the three yearly festivals of Vijayanagar, which will claim attention in connection with other travellers. He describes various funeral and mourning ceremonies, and mentions the significant fact that pestilence was unknown in India. Finally he gives an account of the peculiar, almost Platonic,† system of polyandry prevailing on the Malabar coast, and especially at Calicut, the discussion of which is postponed till it can be dealt with in connection with tra-

* The well-known "hook-swinging."

† Compare Plato, *Republic*, Book v.

vellers possessing fuller and more accurate information. Taking all circumstances into account, our verdict upon Nicolo de' Conti must be that he is an exceedingly valuable witness for the condition of Southern India in the fifteenth century; that while the narrative of Hieronimo di Santo Stefano is quite negligible, and that of Nikitin of comparatively slight value, the loss of Conti's story would have been an irreparable loss. How much Poggio contributed to its superiority must be left undecided; but it is exceedingly possible that the skilful questioning of a cultivated intellect such as that of the Pope's famous secretary rescued his narrative from the jejune barrenness of the accounts of both of the other two travellers; and gave us in its stead an account packed full of facts of the highest significance. No amount of questioning could have rendered the narrative of Hieronimo at all valuable as a source of information, for he saw little of India beyond its ports; but with Nikitin the case is different. From hints he lets drop it seems clear that he was compelled temporarily to abandon the Christian faith, and confess Islam*; it is a thousand pities that he did not, like Conti, seek absolution from his Church, and receive a penance calculated to be so eminently useful to posterity.

* "Now Christian brethren of Russia, whoever of you wishes to go to the Indian country may leave his faith in Russia, confess Mahomet, and then proceed to the land of Hindustan." This, and all preceding quotations from Nikitin are from the translation in *India in the Fifteenth Century* (Hak. Soc.)

CHAPTER III

The Coming of the Portuguese

The travels of the sage of ancient Greece
Or pious Trojan shall not fix our gaze;
Great Alexander should for ever cease
In all the world, nor Trajan's glittering blaze
Resplendent shine, for I will chant the praise
Of Lusian chiefs.

—*Camoens' "Lusiad," I, iii.**

The discovery of America and that of a passage to the East Indies by the Cape of Good Hope are the two greatest and most important events recorded in the history of mankind.—*Adam Smith.*

ON July 8, 1497, the whole population of Lisbon was gathered on the banks of the Tagus. In their midst stood an endless procession of priests in long robes. The gaze of the whole multitude was riveted upon the harbour where the four vessels of the Indian expedition lay waiting the word of command. Suddenly a sound of priests chanting anthems was borne upon the air; the huge concourse took up the refrain as one man; and to the inspiration of the melody preparations for the start were made, the sails were spread to the wind, and the expedition of Vasco da Gama dropped slowly out to sea. Ten months later it cast anchor before the

* Duff's Translation.

port of Calicut. A sea route to India had been discovered, and the change which was to revolutionise the course of the main stream of the world's commerce had begun. The long watchings of Prince Henry the Navigator had at last borne abundant fruit, though he himself had not lived to see the fulfilment of his dreams.

To Vasco da Gama, for his courageous and skilful conduct of the enterprise, unbounded credit is due. But the glory of the exploit itself, of the discovery of an ocean route to India, he must share with a countryman of his own. The honour for its practical discovery is Vasco da Gama's alone; that for its theoretical discovery belongs to Pedro Covilham. In 1487, about the time that Bartholomew Diaz was rounding the Cape of Good Hope, the same desire which had prompted the expedition of Diaz led John the Second of Portugal to despatch Pedro Covilham and Alfonso de Payva overland to India to make careful inquiries into the source of the Venetian commerce in drugs and spices, to discover the far-famed country of Prester John, and to ascertain whether there was any knowledge in India of a sea route round the south coast of Africa between Europe and the East Indies. "They gave them," says Purchas, "a sea-card, taken out of a general map of the world, . . . and all was done very secretly in the house of Peter di Alcazova, and all . . . showed the uttermost of their knowledge as though . . .

in those seas there had been some knowledge of a passage into our western seas, because, the said doctors said, they had found some memoriall of the matter."* It would be tempting but fruitless to speculate what this "memoriall of the matter" can have been. At all events, the travellers started, relying on their information, but at Aden they separated, Payva in order to go to Suakim, Covilham to continue his journey to India. Crossing the Indian Ocean Covilham reached Cannanore, and subsequently Calicut and Goa, being the first Portuguese to sail on the Indian Ocean. Having prosecuted his enquiries here he returned to Cairo, touching Sofala on the way. At Cairo he received letters to the effect that Payva had been murdered. Covilham at once sent to John a report that "the ships which sailed down the coast of Guinea might be sure of reaching the termination of the Continent by persisting in a course to the south; and that when they should arrive in the Eastern Ocean their best direction must be to inquire for Sofala and the Island of the Moon."

Covilham's subsequent travels in Abyssinia, the land of "Prester John," are irrelevant to the subject of this essay. Of his Indian expedition he kept a journal which has unfortunately, as already stated,† disappeared. From the third

* *Purchas his Pilgrimes*, vol. II, p. 1091.

† p. 28, above.

volume of Bruce's Travels we learn that in it he described all the ports and princes of India, with the temper and disposition of the latter, and asserted that the country was populous and full of rich and powerful cities. He also, according to Bruce, asserted that the Cape of Good Hope was well known in India, and appended to his letter a Moorish map of the Cape and its cities.* Covilham is of course of no value as evidence for the condition of India at the time of his visit, owing to the fact that his journal has been lost; but he has been mentioned at this length partly because he was a real traveller, but mainly because the history of his journey shows conclusively that the expedition of Vasco da Gama was by no means such a venture of faith as that of Columbus. Covilham deserves far more of the credit for the discovery of an ocean route to India than has been apportioned him by posterity.

"When the Portuguese," says Sir George Birdwood, "at last, rounding the Cape of Good Hope, burst into the Indian Ocean like a pack of hungry wolves upon a well-stocked sheep-walk, they found a peaceful and prosperous commerce, that had been elaborated during 3,000 years by the Phœnicians and Arabs, being carried on along all its shores."† A few short

* Dr Vincent (*Periplus*, p. 197) ridicules the idea of this "Moorish" map of the South of Africa.

† *Report on the Old Records*, etc., p. 165.

years of violence and conquest were sufficient to destroy this almost as though it had never been, and to transfer its profits to the monopolising and greedy grasp of the Portuguese King. Of the existence of this perennial stream of intercourse between Europe and India, the course of which his discovery was destined to divert for more than three centuries, Vasco da Gama was soon apprised. Almost the first words which the discoverers heard on their arrival at Calicut was the abrupt address in Castilian of two Moorish traders from Tunis: "May the Devil take thee! What brought you hither?" We can imagine the amazement of the voyagers on finding themselves spoken to in their own language so far from home. The remark of the author of the *Roteiro** is not surprising: "We were greatly astonished to hear this talk, for we never expected to hear our language spoken so far away from Portugal." The details of the proceedings of Vasco da Gama during this his first visit to Calicut may be read in this *Roteiro*, in the *Lendas* of Gaspar Correa, in Castanheda and other Portuguese historians, or, for the more poetically inclined, in the *Lusiad* of the poet Camoens. These details are frequently amusing. Gama and those who accompanied him firmly believed the people of India to be Christians. Under this prepossession the author of the *Roteiro* remarks of

* An anonymous journal of the first voyage of Vasco da Gama, published by the Hakluyt Society.

the people of Calicut that " some of them have big beards and long hair, whilst others clip their hair short or shave the head, merely allowing a tuft to remain on the crown as a sign that they are Christians." One may, too, without being guilty of irreverence, be permitted a smile at the picture of Gama and his companions going solemnly to " Mass " in a Hindu temple, under the impression that it was a Christian church, and the side remark of João de Sá, as he knelt by the side of Gama: " If these be devils, I worship the true God."* The scene irresistibly recalls Abu-l-Fazl's famous inscription which so admirably sums up Akbar's eclectic religion, though none would have been sooner to reject it with scorn than the devout men who were at that moment living though unwitting witnesses to its truth. " They threw holy water over us," says the author of the *Roteiro*, " and gave us some white earth, which the Christians of this country are in the habit of putting on their foreheads, breasts, around the neck, and on the forearms. They threw holy water upon the captain-major,† and gave him some of the earth, which he gave in charge of someone, giving them to understand that he would put it on later."‡

During his stay at Calicut a horse was brought to Vasco da Gama, that he might ride on it to his lodgings. According to the custom

* *Castenheda*, p. 57. † i.e., Vasco da Gama. ‡ *Roteiro*, p. 54.

of the district, it was devoid of a saddle, and the Portuguese leader, with that haughtiness which afterwards characterised the dealings of the Portuguese with the natives, suspected a deliberate slight, and refused to mount it.*

Finally, after a short stay, bickerings and quarrels ensued, due principally to the hostile machinations of the Moorish traders at Calicut, and eventually Gama left for Portugal, carrying with him six native gentlemen as trophies, and, in spite of the double dealing which had taken place on both sides, a friendly letter to the King of Portugal, the tenor of which was as follows: "Vasco da Gama, a gentleman of your household, came to my country, whereat I was pleased. My country is rich in cinnamon, cloves, ginger, pepper and precious stones. That which I ask of you in exchange is gold, silver, corals, and scarlet cloth." In September, 1499, amid a pæan of congratulations from his royal master and the populace alike, Vasco da Gama cast anchor in the Tagus, two years after his departure upon his epoch-making voyage; and the curtain fell upon the first act of the tragedy of the Portuguese Empire in Asia.

The following half-century saw the rise of the Portuguese power. All whom the little kingdom could spare, both soldiers and traders, were dispatched to consolidate its hold upon its Eastern Empire, which, as far as theory went,

* *Roteiro*, p. 60.

was one of the greatest that has ever existed. In the words of Pope Alexander the Sixth, the King of Portugal was " Lord of the Navigation, Conquests, and Trade of Ethiopia, Arabia, Persia, and India." Goa speedily became the capital. A succession of famous viceroys, including the great Dalboquerque, some merely capable, some merely cruel, most of them both, extended the power of Portugal throughout the East Indies. Gradually Malacca, Mangalore, Surat, all the Guzerat ports, Muscat, Ormuz, Daman, Calicut, Cochin, most of Ceylon, Negapatam, Bombay, Tatta on the Indus, Masulipatam, Macao, most of the Coromandel and Bengal ports, in fact almost every place of importance to the Indian trade between Aden and Formosa, fell into their hands or beneath their influence. In India itself there was no power capable of resisting their steady advance. Internecine struggle and racial and religious antagonism prevented any common resistance to the invader. The quarrel between the ports of Calicut and Cochin gave the Portuguese their first foothold on the Malabar coast. The long-standing dispute between the kingdom of Vijayanagar and his Mohammedan foes in the Deccan not only nullified all idea of the inhabitants of Southern India making common cause, but so far from this, actually suggested to the Portuguese the formation of an alliance between themselves and the Hindu kingdom against their foes at Calicut and Bijapur. In the north there had long ceased to be a kingdom of Hindustan. The might of Ala-ud-Din-Khilji and Mohammed Taghlak was quite forgotten; and though the vigorous policy of some of the Lodis of Delhi had to some slight extent rescued that ancient kingdom from the degradation of the opening years of the fifteenth century, Hindustan was still only a collection of small states, Mohammedan and Hindu, always seeking to encroach upon one another, as it had been in the days of Conti. Only in the Mohammedan part of the Deccan peninsula had any vital change taken place, and this had been still further dissolution and not the amalgamation which India so much needed. At the coming of Vasco da Gama the great Bahmani kingdom, the predominant power in the Deccan during the fifteenth century, was in process of rapid disintegration. The Adil Shahs, with whom the Portuguese came at first into frequent conflict, had shaken off the Bahmani yoke in 1489 and had established at Bijapur a dynasty which lasted till Aurangzib subverted it in 1686. The Imad Shahs of Berar had made themselves independent in 1484. Six years later Ahmednagar had seen the foundation of the dynasty of the Nizam Shahs. The Barid Shahs of Bidar had rebelled in 1492. Fourteen years after Vasco da Gama's arrival the Kutb Shahs of Golconda followed their example, and the disruption was complete. Mahmud Shah died in 1518, and with him the Bahmanid power came to an end, though during the following eight years three sons and a grandson grasped at the shadow of a throne after the reality had passed away, and proclaimed themselves kings of the magnificent empire which the nerveless hands of their predecessors had been unable to retain. In the meantime the disintegration of Mohammedan power in the Deccan had resulted in the transference of the position of predominant kingdom of South India from the Bahmani empire to Vijayanagar; and though it was not until 1520 that the victory of the latter at Raichur enabled it to enter upon the epoch of its crowning glory, it was to their trade and friendship with Vijayanagar that the early prosperity of the Portuguese in their commerce with South India was, both before and after that event, in no small measure due.

During the seventy or eighty years that succeeded the first voyage of Vasco da Gama to India a number of travellers visited India and left accounts of varying value. The majority of these writers shed light mainly on two kingdoms, that of Vijayanagar and that of Calicut. Though the earliest of these came to India some sixty years before the latest, they yet fall naturally into the same category, and call for collective attention. One only of the famous travellers during the rise of the Portuguese

Empire in Asia cannot be classed in this category; and it therefore seems advisable to close this chapter with an account of the travels of this one exception, and devote a subsequent chapter to the elucidation of the value of the other travellers as evidence for Vijayanagar and the ports (chiefly Calicut) on the Malabar coast. This arrangement will be the more suitable as Mendez Pinto, the traveller referred to, throws light in his narrative rather on the doings of the Portuguese than on the condition, political or social, of the natives of the country, and thus the present chapter will be confined to those who, while immensely famous as travellers or discoverers, give us but little information on the nature and influence of Indian Governments, or on the social institutions of the people, while the next will be devoted to those whose evidence for native India is indispensable, though their fame as adventurers is somewhat less than that of men like Vasco da Gama or Mendez Pinto.

Mendez Pinto has been described above as "famous." "Notorious" is the word which critics have preferred to apply to him ever since his book appeared.* Every writer, with one or two exceptions, has dubbed Mendez Pinto a liar. The wits in popular talk contemptuously changed Mendez into "Mendax." The extent to which the feeling at one time rose can

* A.D. 1614.

be gauged from the fact that Congreve could rely on being understood when in his play, *Love for Love*, he said: "Ferdinand Mendez Pinto was but a type of thee, thou liar of the first magnitude."* It is by no means clear that this condemnation is justified. Pinto certainly is not above embellishing his narrative with picturesque exaggerations; but to damn him as an unmitigated impostor, as almost all have done, is to go too far. Faria y Sousa, the Spanish historian, regarded him as veracious; while his latest editor stoutly maintains Pinto's innocence of the graver charges brought against him. "Marco Polo," says Monsieur A. Vambéry, "the Prince of Asiatic travellers, who was not renowned for apostolic zeal, was rewarded only with sneers and mockery for his great and fruitful work, and for centuries Italy designated a liar and boaster with the expression 'Marco Millioni.' A like fate befell the famous Portuguese, Fernao Mendez Pinto, who between the years 1537–1558 journeyed through the most difficult parts of Asia, and during his twenty-one years' wanderings, as he himself says, was sold sixteen times, was a slave thirteen times, and was shipwrecked five times."† If we may believe his account he travelled widely in almost all the countries known as the "East Indies."

* Act ii, Scene 5.

† *The Voyages and Adventures of Fernao Mendez Pinto* (abridged), 1891. Introduction by M. A. Vambéry.

mainly by sea or on the coasts, and underwent an extraordinary series of adventures. The origin of the disbelief with which the world greeted his narrative is to be found in the fact that the description which Pinto gives of the fearful atrocities and inhuman lust for blood which characterised the conduct of the Portuguese in their subversion of the overland trade route were simply incredible. Pinto's account of Portuguese cruelty was, it must be admitted, too horrible to be believed; and yet we know from other sources that it had at least a substratum of truth. Camoens, in his *Lusiad*, depicted the noble aspirations and high moral and spiritual aims with which the Portuguese set forth on their career of empire in India; Pinto painted another aspect of the picture. Both men exaggerated, the one, as a true poet must, in the direction of idealism; the other, like the sensationalist he was, in the direction of realism; but even when we make allowance for the opposite tendencies of the two writers, the contrast between them is sufficiently sharp to form one of the saddest features in Indo-European history. The Portuguese Empire in Asia has been referred to as a tragedy; it was also a satire on human nature.*

* The most convenient book in which the subject of the present chapter may be more fully studied is *The Portuguese in India*, by Mr F. C. Danvers, which has been frequently consulted in the composition of this work.

CHAPTER IV

The Evidence for Southern India of Portuguese and Italian Travellers (1500-80)

Then Happy they who quit their private Home
And gen'rously through foreign climates roam;
Who, like Ulysses, can despise the toil,
And make each Land they meet their Native soil.

—*N. Tate.*

THE travellers from whose narratives the bulk of the present chapter is derived are five in number—Ludovico di Varthema, Duarte Barbosa, Caesar de Federici, Fernao Nuniz, and Domingos Paes. Some additional evidence has been obtained from the *Commentaries of the Great Afonso Dalboquerque*,* and Camoens' *Lusiad*. Other narratives exist and have been consulted, but their value is in the main slight.† The evidence of these men is important from several distinct points of view. For information on the habits and political condition of the people of the Malabar coast, Varthema, Barbosa (or whoever may have been the author of the work which goes under his name), and Federici, are absolutely indispensable; other less important writers con-

* Hak. Soc. Publication.

† e.g., the narratives of Corsali, Empoli, and Lopez, in Ramusio.

tain some evidence, though it only tells us ineffectively what the three already mentioned tell us well. For Vijayanagar and its condition under the second dynasty, the three are likewise valuable; but from this point of view they must yield pride of place to Nuniz and Paes, without whose narratives it is not overemphatic to assert that the history of Vijayanagar cannot be written. As a rule the narratives of the European travellers are only the flesh and blood which help to make the historical skeleton a living thing; for the history of Vijayanagar Nuniz and Paes provide a considerable portion of the dry bones as well. Notices of towns on the Coromandel coast, of Guzerat, the Concan, Orissa and Bengal, and the Mohammedan kingdoms of the Deccan, especially Bijapur, are fairly frequent in Barbosa and one or two other writers, but hardly demand special attention at this point, as the evidence of later travellers about these districts is fuller and more exact. Their evidence is valuable chiefly in connection with Calicut and Vijayanagar, and it is in this aspect that they will be, in the main, discussed. The detailed analysis, however, of their information may conveniently be prefaced by a sketch of their travels.

Camoens and Dalboquerque* need not

* It is perhaps hardly necessary to remind the reader that the "Commentaries," which are an account of Dalboquerque's life in India, were written, not by the Viceroy, but by his natural son, Braz Dalboquerque.

delay us. The great viceroy was one of the founders of the Portuguese power in Asia, and was in the east during parts of the first and second decades of the century; Camoens travelled in the East Indies between 1553 and 1569. The history of the one is part of the history of his country; the history of the other belongs to the history of his country's literature. For this reason, as well as because both are partially or wholly excluded by the criterion laid down in the first chapter, and all reference to them is merely incidental, a further account of these two famous men is unnecessary.

Ludovico di Varthema was a native of Bologna. He travelled not only in India, but in almost all the countries on the overland route thither, and wrote a record of his observations which has been so appreciated that it has at various times been translated from the original Italian into five other modern languages as well as into Latin. He travelled not with a view to political or commercial possibilities, like the majority of our travellers, but for travel's sake. His motives were twofold, curiosity and ambition; curiosity to see, ambition for the renown of having seen. He visited India just before the Portuguese had obtained a firm footing in the country, and one of the most valuable portions of his narrative is that in which he sketches the state of the overland trade in the days before the discovery of an ocean route to India had had time greatly to affect it.

Varthema left Europe at the end of 1502, and, travelling via Cairo, Beirut, Damascus, and Mecca, reached Aden by a voyage down the Red Sea. At Aden he was thrown into prison as a Christian spy. After effecting his escape by means of an intrigue with the queen of that city, Varthema made his way to the north-east coast of Africa, whence he sailed to Diu in Guzerat. He now altered his direction, and crossed the Indian Ocean to Ormuz. After a visit to Herat, Varthema returned to the port and took ship to "Cheo" (Kow) and Cambay. Of Cambay he gives a very fair description, mentioning the religious scruples of the Guzerates which prevented them eating flesh or killing anything which possessed life. They are, he asserts, neither Moors nor "Gentoos," but he thinks that if they were baptised their many good works would ensure their salvation. This excessive goodness of theirs had rendered them the prey of "Machamuth,"* their present king, who was of an opposite disposition. The traveller's description of this monarch is diverting. His mustachios were so long that he tied them over his head as a woman would tie her tresses, while his beard reached to his girdle.

* Mahmud Shah Begara, King of Guzerat, 1459–1511 A.D. The original of Butler's "Prince of Cambay," whose "daily food is asp, and basilisk and toad." See Elphinstone's *History*, ninth edition, p. 743. *Oriental Biog. Dict.* p. 232.

Varthema retails, in perfect good faith, some extraordinary stories of his betel-chewing propensities.

Sailing southwards, Varthema touched at "Cevul" (Chaul), Dabul, "Onor,"* and Mangalore, at which last port he struck inland in order to visit Vijayanagar. After visiting the Hindu capital, he made his way to Calicut, which at that time rivalled Cambay for the dignity of being the greatest port in India. The traveller's description of Calicut occupies a third of his work and is very valuable. His information was obtained at first hand by intimate association with the natives. Varthema now left Calicut, and after touching at Quilon and the island of Ceylon, which he mentions as being the theatre of internecine combats between four rival kings, visited Pulicat, Negapatam, "Tarnasseri," and "Banghella." In his subsequent travels to Pegu, Malacca, Sumatra, and Borneo, we need not follow him; but one significant discovery of his cannot be omitted. He tells us that on this voyage he heard some rumours of a land to the south, and of a very cold place where the day only lasted four hours. So early a reference as this to Australia and the Antarctic Circle, which were destined to remain undiscovered for many years to come, is of more than ordinary interest. On his return to India Varthema was present at a great sea-fight

* Honavar.

between the Portuguese and the Samorin's fleet off Cannanore. After becoming a factor at Cochin he was subsequently made a knight by the Viceroy, Almeida. In 1507 he finally left for Europe, returning home by the Cape route on a Portuguese ship. Varthema closes his account of his travels with a brief retrospect of the doings of the Portuguese in the East, and foretells for them a brilliant future.

In Varthema's record the personality of the man is everything; in that of the next of our travellers, Duarte Barbosa, it does not count. Indeed, it is not by any means certain that Barbosa was the author of the treatise which bears his name, and purports to be a description of his travels. This is not the place to enter upon an elaborate examination of Barbosa's claims to its authorship; but a few facts must be stated. The choice seems to lie between Barbosa, its reputed author, and the great discoverer, Magellan. Both these two men went to India in the early days of the Portuguese settlements in the East Indies. Magellan returned to Europe in 1512; Barbosa followed suit, it seems, though it is not clear, in 1517. When Magellan in 1519 triumphantly passed through the straits which now bear his name, and so discovered a western route to India, he was accompanied by Barbosa. The Hakluyt Society Translator* of these Travels, which were entitled *A Description*

* Lord Stanley of Alderley.

of the Coasts of East Africa and Malabar, inclined to reject the authorship of Barbosa, which Ramusio supported, and to assign the work to Magellan. Chief among his reasons for this conclusion was the fact that although Barbosa was in India in 1508–9 the author of this narrative describes the naval actions of those years at Diu as one only. He suggested that " the volumes were drawn up by Magellan, or under Magellan's guidance, for the purpose of being laid before Charles V at the time that Magellan was seeking the commission which he received a short time later." He regarded the book, not as the record of a single traveller, but as a sort of eclectic description of India and East Africa gathered from the reports and stories of the various Portuguese traders who travelled in those regions in the early days of the Portuguese empire in the East. He based this conclusion partly on the large number of places which the author, if he drew his account entirely from personal observation, must have visited. " It is difficult to imagine that one person visited all the places described in this volume, even in the space of sixteen years, at a period when travelling was slower than at present, and the observations on the manners and customs show a more intimate knowledge than what could be acquired by touching at a port for a few days only." In India proper, for instance, Guzerat, the Mohammedan kingdom of the Deccan, Vijayanagar, Malabar, the kingdom of "Hotisa," with their respective towns, are described with fair minuteness; outside the Peninsula Pegu, the islands of the Archipelago, and the East African coast, are equally well done. If the above theory was right, as on the face of it seems quite possible, and the reputed narrative of Duarte Barbosa is only an eclectic compilation, and not a personal record, it robs the author, whoever he may have been, of much of his credit as a traveller, though it in no way detracts from the usefulness of his information.

During the first half century of the Portuguese empire in India, their trade with Vijayanagar was of considerable importance to them. In consequence we hear of a number of Portuguese going there in one capacity or another. Perhaps the best known of them is Fray Luis, who was sent there by Dalboquerque in 1509, in order to conclude an agreement between the Portuguese and the King of Vijayanagar, but was somewhat mysteriously murdered.* Two men who went there as traders have left us valuable accounts of their observations. One was Domingos Paes, who wrote his account about the year 1520; the other was Fernao Nuniz, who went there probably some ten or fifteen years later. These two

* *Commentaries of Afonso Dalboquerque* (Hakluyt Society Edition, ii, p. 71; iii, p. 35–38). Fray Luis travelled from Cochin via Bhatkal to Vijayanagar. We are told that a Turk killed him by the orders of the King of Bijapur.

documents were sent, as Mr Sewell, their English translator, says,* "by some one at Goa to some one in Europe." The latter was almost certainly the historian Barros, who used the chronicles in compiling his history. Until recently, however, they had been forgotten, and, in fact, were never published at all till Senhor Lopes in 1897 issued a Portuguese edition at Lisbon,† and so helped the world to gain a better knowledge of what Mr Sewell only too rightly termed "A Forgotten Empire." Paes's chronicle is valuable chiefly because he describes what he saw at the great Hindu capital with fidelity and truth; that of Nuniz because he gives a summary of the previous history of the kings of Vijayanagar, traditional only, it is true, but gathered at first hand upon the spot, and the best that was attainable. The record of Paes is that of a sightseer; that of Nuniz is practically an amateur history of Vijayanagar. As a basis for the history of Vijayanagar Nuniz is absolutely indispensable; for its institutions during the last fifty years of its existence as a great kingdom Paes is equally valuable. Both are far more graphic and detailed than Conti or Varthema. Referring to the great capital, the writer of the covering letter which accompanied the chronicles to Barros

* Page v of Introduction to *A Forgotten Empire* (*Vijayanagar*).

† *Chronica dos Reis de Bisnaga*, by David Lopes, S.S.G.L., Lisbon, 1897; at the National Press. Mr Sewell's English translation appeared in 1900, forming part of his work, *A Forgotten Empire* (*Vijayanagar*).

said: "I know no one goes there without bringing away his quire of papers about its affairs." It is to be deplored that others of these accounts have not survived, but it is probable that these two were superior to the rest, as the writer of the covering letter had been specially asked by Barros to obtain for him some account of Vijayanagar, and would naturally send the historian the best he could find.

The last of the travellers of this period was Caesar de Federici, or, as he is known in the pages of Purchas, Caesar Frederick. He was an Italian, and travelled in the East from 1563 to 1581. "In the yeer of our Lord God, 1563," runs Purchas's version, "I, Caesar Frederick, being in Venice, and very desirous to see the East parts of the world, took my journey to Alepo." Reaching Ormuz by the usual route, he went by ship to Diu, "situate in a little island in the Kingdome of Cambaya, which is the greatest strength that the Portugals have in all the Indies, yet a small city, but of great trade." He mentions the fact that when he was there a great famine was raging, and the people were selling their children to the Portuguese for ten shillings apiece. In 1567 Caesar de Federici was at Goa, whence he travelled inland to Vijayanagar, which had been sacked two years before by the combined power of the Mohammedan kings of the Deccan. He gives a melancholy picture of the ruined greatness of the mighty city: "The city of Bezeneger is not altogether destroyed, yet the houses stand still, but emptie, and there is dwelling in them nothing, as is reported, but Tygres and other wild beasts." The vaunting insolence* of the "Kafir" Kings had been repaid with interest, and Vijayanagar had ceased for ever from among the cities of the world. More than three fourths of a century were destined to elapse before the rise of the next champion of Hindu nationality against Mohammedan oppression. For three hundred years Vijayanagar had been the means of saving part of Southern India for Hinduism, but the task she had imposed upon herself had at last proved too much for her.

From the ruined city Caesar de Federici returned to Goa, and then journeyed to Cochin, "next unto Goa the chiefest place of the Portugals." Of the Nairs of this city he gives some interesting details. Following this he went to Quilon, and after touching at Ceylon, seems to have gone on to Negapatam, St Thome, Orissa, Bengal, Pegu, and a number of other places beyond India proper. Federici returned to Ormuz in 1580, and finally reached Venice in 1581.

From these travellers information of varying value can be obtained on almost all the countries

* e.g. After the battle of Raichur Krishna Deva Raya demanded degrading terms of peace from his enemy the Adil Shah of Bijapur. See Sewell, *A Forgotten Empire (Vijayanagar)*, p. 156, 157.

on the sea border of India proper, and on many of the inland kingdoms of Southern India; but, as has been intimated before, it is only in connection with the kingdoms of Calicut and Vijayanagar that a detailed analysis of their accounts repays the trouble. It will be convenient first to review their evidence for Calicut.

When Vasco da Gama reached India in 1498 he found that Calicut, the name of which port was well known in Europe, was the greatest commercial city in Southern India. Upon the profits derived from its prominent position in the commercial world its king had grown rich, and the city, which was one of a number of city states along the Malabar coast, had grown powerful; while, that the goose which was responsible for the golden eggs might not be strangled, moderate customs, absolute religious toleration, and perfect security of person and property, were the fortunate lot of the foreign merchants at Calicut. The natural result had followed. To quote the words which Camoens put into the mouth of a Moslem speaker,

> Wealth has flowed
> From commerce with the world, in heaps they pile
> All that the seas can bring from China and the Nile.*

The Samorin of Calicut was perfectly sincere, in all probability, in his protestations of friendship and welcome to the Portuguese on their

* Duff's Translation.

first arrival, as it was clearly to his advantage that there should be as many channels as possible by which Asiatic products might reach Europe. It was only the intrigues of the Moorish traders, who were bound to be hard hit by Portuguese competition, that caused him to change his friendly tactics. Camoens has a verse that admirably sums up his attitude:

> But should you have the wish in merchandize
> With us to trade, this fertile land is blessed
> With all the richest wares the East supplies,
> Cloves, cinnamon, and spices of the best,
> Most potent drugs whose virtues all attest:
> If then for precious stones your bosom pants,
> Of rubies rare, and diamonds we 're possessed,
> In heaps; nor deem these boasts, or idle vaunts,
> Our rich and ample store by far exceeds your wants.*

Varthema is very clear as to the excellent conditions under which trade was carried on at Calicut before the arrival of the Portuguese. He tells us there was a fixed customs duty at the place of entry or of embarkation; and the perfect freedom from petty persecution, which it is clear from his narrative they enjoyed, contrasts favourably with the treatment later on meted out to the early traders in the land of the "Great Mogul," of which mention will be made later.

As regards the internal administration of the city, our attention is first drawn to the legal system in force there. On its impartiality

* ii, 4, Duff's Translation.

Varthema is enthusiastic. If the scales of Justice are heavy, she yet holds them evenly. Such at least is the general impression derived from Varthema's account. Duarte Barbosa is less eulogistic, and supplies a necessary corrective both of Varthema and of his Hakluyt Society editor.* From Barbosa we obtain the salient fact that justice was administered "according to the qualities of the persons." The system doubtless worked well, and, having regard to all the circumstances, was perhaps the best possible; but it surely does not call for enthusiasm. In Calicut nobles enjoyed privilege. They could not be arrested or put in irons for any offence whatever. If a noble does wrong, "they call up three or four gentlemen in whom the king places confidence, and he bids them go and kill the noble, and they give them a warrant from the king to do so. And then they lay him on his back, and pin the warrant on his chest, and leave him there."

So far so good. If rough and ready, it was at least speedy and effective—no small merit in legal affairs—though it is not clear that an accused noble had any opportunity of offering a defence to the charge, but might be set upon in the street and executed without being made aware of his alleged offence. But, on reading further, we descend at once, if not from the

* *The Travels of Ludovico di Varthema*, edited for the Hakluyt Society by Rev. George Percy Badger.

sublime, at least from the moderately sensible, to the ridiculous. "When a noble accuses a noble," says Barbosa, "they have ordeal by boiling butter." The same absurdity which Conti had remarked in the Hindu parts of Southern India was still to be found at Calicut and, no doubt, elsewhere on the Malabar coast and in the interior. On this, at least, the civilising influence of the Moorish traders had had no effect.

As to the lower classes, their lot was pitiable. "If any low people commits a robbery, if they find the thing stolen in his hand, or if he confess, if he is a gentile, they execute him. They set some high posts with sharp points and small stand, and they cut off his head with a sword, and spit him through the back and pit of the stomach. The point comes out a cubit and on it they spit his head. They then tie ropes to his legs and arms, and fasten them to four posts, so that the limbs are stretched out and the body on its back upon the stand."* In like circumstances a Moor had the privilege of being stabbed instead of being beheaded, but the goods stolen became the property of the governor. If, on the other hand, the thief neither confessed nor was taken *in flagrante delicto*, boiling oil, or, in the case of a Moor, a red-hot axe, was brought into requisition. If the application of these did no injury to the

* *Barbosa*, Hak. Soc. edition, p. 116.

accused, he was acquitted. In the case of a very slight offence, a fine was inflicted, or the culprit was sold as a slave, the proceeds in either case going to the governor. In the case of women offenders, fines alone were inflicted, death never. If a woman of noble family offended against the law of her sect, the king usually ordered her to be sold as a slave, a sentence which her relations, to avoid disgrace, generally, with the full approval of the king, prevented being carried out by killing her.

Varthema gives an interesting account of the proper ritual for the recovery of debt, which is well worth quoting. " Let us suppose," he says, " the case that someone has to pay me twenty-five ducats, and the debtor promises me to pay them many times, and does not pay them; I, not being willing to wait any longer, nor to give him any indulgence, shall take a green branch in my hand, shall go softly behind the debtor, and with the said branch shall draw a circle on the ground surrounding him, and if I can enclose him in the circle, I shall say to him these words three times: 'Bramini raza pertha polle,' *i.e.*, I command you by the head of the Brahmins and of the king, that you do not depart hence until you have paid me and satisfied me as much as I ought to have from thee. And he will satisfy me or truly he will die there without any other guard. And should he quit the said circle and not pay me, the king would put him to death." Edrisi of Sicily who was in India in the twelfth century,* also mentions this custom, and it seems to have been the common ritual on the Malabar coast for the recovery of a debt. All things considered, the administration of justice at Calicut had by the sixteenth century been reduced to a system to an extent which surprises us, and well repays examination, though it by no means merits the eulogies which have been lavished upon it by certain writers.

As regards social customs two things seem to have struck all observers. The first was the tyranny to which caste convention attained in Calicut; the other the polyandry of the Nair women.

The first phenomenon has been well put in the *Lusiad* in a single verse:

> For those who exercised a craft or trade
> Must not with other castes in marriage blend,
> The same injunction on their children laid
> Compels them in that trade their lives to spend
> From earliest childhood to their final end.
> The Nairs vile shame and great disgrace endure
> If any Pariah should by touch offend
> Their noble flesh, and force them to procure
> A thousand remedies, to make them clean and pure.†

Varthema and Barbosa both give lists of the sects at Calicut. The highest was that of the Brahmins. Next came the Nairs, who were obliged to bear a sword and shield or bow and

* See above, page 15.

† *Lusiad*, VII, 38 (Duff's Translation).

lance when going through the street. According to Varthema, who is the better authority, these were followed in order by the "Tiva" or artisans, the "Mechua" or Fisherman, and the "Poliar" and the "Hirava," who were agriculturists. These latter were bound not to come within fifty paces of a Brahmin or a Nair, unless called by them; and when going along the street were obliged to call aloud "Popo," to warn them; for if they suddenly met a Brahmin or a Nair, they could be killed with impunity for defiling them.*

In the kingdom of Calicut the woman, not the man, was the stock of inheritance. Thus the direct successor of the king was his sister's son, not his own. This remarkable custom was due to the extraordinary marriage conventions prevalent among the Nairs of the Malabar towns. By collating the accounts given by various, among them later,† travellers, we gather that the Nairs married before the age of ten, but never permanently cohabited with their wives. The wife lived with her mother or brother, and received whom she would of high rank. The system was practically polyandry, as the number of Nairs admitted was in practice strictly limited, and each of them contributed to the upkeep of the wife. The chil-

* *The Travels of Ludovico di Varthema* (Hak. Soc.), p. 142.

† The best account given by any traveller is perhaps that of Dr Buchanan in *Pinkerton's Collection*, VIII, p. 737. Cp. also *Ibn Batuta*, Lee (167).

dren were apportioned according to the wife's directions. Varthema, Federici, and Barbosa all mention the system and the extraordinary law of inheritance resulting from it; but they do not grasp all the details of the system. Federici looks upon it as a community of wives, which it by no means was. It seems to have been only the Nairs among whom this custom obtained. Apart from their marriage conventions these Nairs seem to have been an extraordinary sect. They resemble nothing so much as a military aristocracy. From other travellers we learn that without a paid escort from them it was utterly impossible to travel safely in the country, and that the escort was sufficient, even though it consisted only of one or two Nairs. It was not so much the fighting ability of the escort that provided the defence and secured the traveller's safety as the fact that one of the military caste had been propitiated. The exaction of the impost was the application to individuals of a kind of insurance system, whereby a small proportion of one's property was yielded to ensure the safety of the rest, and in practice probably entailed little real hardship. Among other peculiarities of these Nairs Federici notices the huge ear-holes which were the patent of their nobility. In one which he measured it was possible to insert one's arm up to the shoulder, "clothed as it was."

So much for the kingdom of Calicut. Vijayanagar, or, as the Portuguese called it, "Narsinga," next demands attention. An analysis of the various important references to it in Federici, Varthema, Barbosa, and the two Portuguese traders whose detailed accounts we possess, would require a volume to itself. All that can be attempted here is an outline of the chief features of the picture of the great kingdom which can be synthetised from the various narratives available.

In 1490 the first dynasty of the kings of Vijayanagar came to an end, and Narasimha usurped the throne. It was in his reign that the Portuguese first came into contact with the kingdom, and erroneously imagining the name of the sovereign to be that of the country, applied the name "Narsinga" to the kingdom, and reserved the name "Bisnegar" for the capital. Narasimha was on the throne when Varthema visited the city. He gives seven miles as the circumference of Vijayanagar, considerably reducing the extravagant estimates of earlier travellers.* He, too, however, adds his voice to the chorus of praise and wonder. "The King of Narsinga is the richest king I have ever heard spoken of."

Barbosa—or the traveller from whose observations the account of Vijayanagar in *The Coast of East Africa and Malabar* is drawn—

* e.g., Conti says sixty miles. I do not understand the extravagance of his estimate.

visited the city some time during the early part of the sixteenth century. Whether he went there before the accession of Krishna Deva Raya in 1509 it is impossible to say with certainty. From him we have a graphic description of the great city, with its "very large and handsome palaces," its numerous courts, its houses covered with thatch, its spacious streets and squares, its "infinite trade," and innumerable details beside. He tells us of the king's frequent wars with the "king of Dacani,"* who "has taken from him much of his land." As at Calicut, life and property were secure. In the streets of Vijayanagar there thronged "an innumerable crowd of all nations and creeds; for besides many Moorish merchants and traders, and the Gentile inhabitants of the country who are very rich, an infinite number of others flock there from all parts, who are able to come, dwell, trade, and live very freely, and in security, without anyone molesting them, or asking or requiring of them any account of whence they come, or in what creed they live, whether they be Moors, Christians, or Gentiles . . . . Strict justice and truth are observed towards all." The contrast between the reception accorded to the early traders by these so-called unenlightened "Kafirs" and that accorded by the art-loving civilised Moguls is not to the advantage of the latter. The one grasped

* The Adil Shah of Bijapur.

the true spirit of commercial intercourse and the principles on which it is based; the other, blinded by contempt for trade in general, not only refused to guarantee the safety of the traders' cargoes, but interposed all kinds of petty and hampering restrictions.

As an example of the wisdom of the king Barbosa gives an amusing account of the way in which he chastised high officials who departed from the strict path of duty. It is too long to quote, but it will convey some idea of the principle on which the monarch acted when we say that his object was to punish the official without being compelled to dispense with his services or degrade him in the eyes of the people.*

Federici gives a valuable account of the downfall of Vijayanagar in 1565, and of its condition and that of the country round two years later. Part of his description of the ruined city has been quoted on an earlier page of this chapter.† Federici's narrative includes one of the best of the early descriptions of suttee which we possess, as well as a description of another method "for baser people."‡

From the mass of facts given by Paes and Nuniz, a few only can be mentioned. Paes has a very interesting account of the two great festivals of which he was an eyewitness. One of these was the nine-days' Mahanavami festi-

* See p. 89 of *The Coast of East Africa and Malabar.*
† Above, p. 71. ‡ *Purchas his Pilgrimes*, ii, 1702.

val; the second was the festival of the New Year's day. He also mentions others, and enables us to see the magnificence with which these feasts were kept.* Among other events of the festivals he describes the athletic games which were witnessed by immense crowds of people. The wrestling matches, to judge from his account, seem to have resembled boxing rather than wrestling contests. There were, too, endless processions, dancing, fireworks, and sacrificial rites of all kinds. By way of appendix to his account of the feasts Paes describes the almost incredible revenues of the king, his immense army, amounting to a million troops, and the holocaust of victims offered on important days at the shrine of the idols. From Nuniz, as well as from Paes, we gather that human sacrifices were occasionally consummated on the inauguration of solemn or momentous undertakings, such as that of a great irrigation work.†

Nuniz gives us an interesting sidelight on the condition of the ryots of Southern India. "All the land," he says, "belongs to the king, and from his hand the captains hold it. They make it over to the husbandmen who pay nine-tenths to their lord; and they have no land of their own, for the kingdom belongs entirely to the king."‡ This statement is strong confirmation

* See p.p. 262–275 in Paes' narrative in *A Forgotten Empire*.
† *A Forgotten Empire*, pp. 245, 365.
‡ Nuniz's narrative in *A Forgotten Empire*, p. 379.

of the view commonly held that under the great Hindu Monarchy, no less than elsewhere, the ryots of Southern India suffered almost intolerable economic slavery at the hands of their rulers.

The king, as has generally been the case in India, seems always to have been open to direct petition. In cases of robbery, the captain of the province in which it had taken place was held responsible for the amount of its value until the thief was discovered.* Punishments were homœopathic; if a man stole, his hand was cut off. Among the lower orders all crimes were punished with death. Barbarous methods of inflicting it were common, impaling alive being the usual penalty of treason. Duelling was permitted and encouraged, but permission had first to be obtained from the minister. The victor in a duel took the dead man's estate. For the financial and military organisation of the kingdom, the prevalence of suttee, funeral ceremonies, a graphic account of the battle of Raichur, and numerous other items of historical or social information, the reader may be referred to the narrative itself.

Such is the information which the sixteenth century visitors to Vijayanagar have left us on the Hindu kingdom. Combined with those of the preceding century, these travellers enable us to gain at least a faint idea of the magnifi-

* See Sewell's *A Forgotten Empire*, p. 380.

cence, power, and comparative civilisation of the empire and city which amazed them all. Into the secret of her three hundred years' resistance to the Mohammedan advance they do not greatly initiate us; but at least they enable us to assert that Camoens slandered them when he attributed it to her wealth rather than to the bravery of her sons.* It is "men, high-minded men," as a distinguished Anglo-Indian† once reminded us, that "constitute a state"; and though undoubtedly the wealth which the equity of her institutions deservedly enabled her to obtain was a contributory factor, her success was in the main due to the fire of that Hindu patriotism which native Rajahs kept alive in isolated fastnesses, and which was destined in later years to blaze into flame in the Concan hills. For the history of this faint anticipation of the revival of Hinduism under the Mahrattas, the narratives of the European travellers, as has been said before, are invaluable. As evidence for Calicut they are exceedingly useful, but for Vijayanagar they are indispensable. Mr Sewell used them as the basis of his magnificent and erudite contribution to the history of Southern India, which, in recognition of the pioneer nature of his researches, he well entitled *A Forgotten Empire*. Forgotten, how-

* Great power Narsinga's kingdom always claimed,
But more by gold and precious stones it shone
Than valiant men. —*Lusiad*, VII, 21 (Duff).

† Sir William Jones, "Ode in imitation of Alcæus."

ever, it is no longer, for his patient and comprehensive work has brought together almost every scrap of evidence which exists on the subject. Of this evidence European travellers provide no small proportion.

CHAPTER V

The Portuguese Missionary Travellers

The Portuguese monarchs had always loudly proclaimed, that the diffusion of the Catholic faith, and the extension of the spiritual dominion of the Pope, was a still more favourite aim in all their conquests than even to enlarge the sphere of their own empire. Without inquiring whether their zeal went quite so far, it cannot be denied, that had the legitimacy of the means corresponded to the ardour with which the object was pursued, this claim to praise would have been very ample.—*Hugh Murray.*

THE Church of Rome has never lacked earnest and eager helpers in the prosecution of its missionary enterprises. Least of all has it lacked them in India. Alike in the homely story of the author of the *Roteiro*, and in the elevated imagery of Camoens, we can clearly see that one of the incentives which served to stir the early Portuguese navigators to greater effort was the prospect of a large addition of strength to the Catholic Church. The result was that immediately the Portuguese power was firmly established in the East, missionary friars were despatched in large numbers to convert India to the Christian faith. Of this policy the fruits which remain to-day are two-fold. The one is the greater part of the large

Christian population which exists to-day in India; the other is the undying fame of St Francis Xavier, one of the most famous of all the famous men who have ever served the Church of Rome.

The present is not the proper place either for a sketch of Xavier's life or for a history of Portuguese missions in India. Xavier himself, who first went to India in 1538, is excluded by our canon from all but passing mention in this work. But among that host of humbler men who strove to emulate his inspiring example, there were some who wrote descriptions of their travels which embody a considerable amount of information on the people and places which they visited. As a preliminary to their discussion we may say that with these missionary travellers we reach a time when the main stream of travel begins to direct itself northward, instead of confining itself, as heretofore, mainly to the south.

More than one historian has lamented the fact that though Europeans were frequent visitors to almost the whole of Southern India at the time when Babar and his unlucky son Humayun were on the throne of Delhi, no traveller was adventurous enough to direct his steps in their direction. The consequence is that we are without a picture from European sources of either the sturdy and vigorous conqueror who became the first of the "Great

Moguls," or his ill-starred successor, whose chief claim on the memory of posterity is the fact that he was the father of the most famous and great-hearted monarch who ever sat on an Indian throne. With regard to that remarkable man, who succeeded Humayun in 1556, the fates have been kinder; but even so they have distributed their gifts in niggardly fashion. For one really complete European picture of Akbar we would gladly exchange any number of the sketches that later travellers give us of his less famous son. As it is, we are forced to have recourse to a rather meagre account of that king which can be gathered from the description of the visit of a number of Jesuits to his court.

In 1568, Akbar, who was then about twenty-five years of age, and was already rivalling Marcus Aurelius as the incarnation of Plato's aspiration for the king-philosopher, wrote the Portuguese viceroy at Goa a courteous letter, requesting that priests might be sent to him with the books of the law and the Gospel of Christ. The Archbishop at Goa did not hesitate to avail himself of so brilliant an opportunity of gaining for his missionaries a favourable hearing in the greatest kingdom of North India, and despatched a mission which started at the close of 1569.* Fatepur, where Akbar was then resid-

* The expedition comprised Rodolpho Aquaviva, Antonio de Monserrato, and Francisco Enriques. The first is mentioned by Abu-l-fazl as Padri Radalf (not Redif, as Elphinstone has it), p. 523.

ing, was made their objective. Having reached Surat by sea, they immediately found themselves in a district where customs were quite different from anything which they had previously seen. Chief among the objects which excited their curiosity were the numerous hospitals for lame and sick birds which existed there.

Their narrative contains an amusing account of the way in which the extravagant reverence of the natives for animal life was exploited by a Portuguese captain who was in need of money. Collecting a number of dogs, he announced that he was about to drown them, whereupon the devout in the city subscribed a large sum to prevent the deed. The friars noticed that whilst these numerous hospitals existed for sick birds, human beings were left outside in the streets to perish unheeded. They mention, too, the extreme trickery practised by the usurers and other business men. After crossing the Tapti and the Nerbudda, they proceeded by Mandu, Ujen, Sarangpur, and Seronj, travelling on the way through such dangerous country, and encountering such discomforts, that the reverend fathers take occasion to point out that nothing could console them for their suffering but the hopes of Paradise. At last, at the end of February, they reached Fatepur, and were at once introduced into Akbar's presence. They found him about fifty* years old, as white as a European, and "of sagacious intellect." He greeted them courteously, offered them money, and was pleased when they declined it; and made ample arrangements for their lodging while at Fatepur. A little later a theological contest was arranged by the Emperor between the Christian fathers and some Mohammedan mollahs. Such a dispute could of course have but one ending. A heated discussion took place, at the end of which each party considered he had indubitably proved his case. Akbar listened with courtesy and attention, and at the close said he was well pleased with the Christian religion, though there were some of its mysteries which appeared to him incomprehensible. After a considerable stay, the missionaries called on the king to embrace Christianity and to establish it in his kingdom; and though the Mogul monarch made no definite reply, a courtier allowed it to transpire that Akbar only looked upon the friars as a valuable source of intellectual entertainment, and had no intention of adopting their doctrines. Not unnaturally they were annoyed, but Akbar's unfailing courtesy and his reverence for the picture of the Virgin, kept them continually hopeful. They did not know Akbar as we know him now. They imagined that the

* There is some discrepancy here. Akbar was twenty-eight at the time of the friars' first visit. It is possible that he looked considerably older than his actual age.

great seeker after religious truth, who all his life was searching for light in the various creeds of man, would content himself with one. At this early date, perhaps, he had not fully attained to the eclecticism of his later years. But he was groping toward it. Even now he could say, with his friend Abu-l-Fazl, "O God, in every temple I see those who see thee, and in every tongue that is spoken thou art praised. . . . . Awhile I frequent the Christian cloister, anon the mosque: but Thee only I seek from fane to fane."* But possibly he had not yet decided that there was no one faith which was vastly superior to all other existing creeds. And so he listened eagerly to the message of the Christian friars. Before their arrival, we are told, the king counted the hours and measured every stage, so great was the consuming fire of the spirit of inquiry within him. But then came disenchantment. As friar and mollah argued before him, he saw in his Christian visitors the same angry intolerance, the same universal condemnation, of all outside their pale; objurgation was met with objurgation, abuse countered with abuse;† of that quiet seeking spirit which he loved he saw in them no trace or sign; of their

* From the version in Mr S. Lane-Poole's *Medieval India*, p. 277.

† The uncompromising and hostile attitude of the two contending parties may be gathered from the remark of the historian Badaoni. "These accursed monks," he says, "applied the description of cursed Satan, and of his qualities, to Muhammad, the best of all prophets—God's blessings rest on him and his whole house !—a thing which even devils would not do." See Ain i Akbari, Blochmann, vol. 1, 183.

doctrines, some were mysteries which he could not understand, but all else was, as Tennyson so well put it, " Form, Ritual, varying with the tribes of Men."* The expanding soul, which had long passed beyond the bounds of Islam, could not confine itself within the limits of the faith of these visitors from the West. But, in season and out of season alike, the hopeful missionaries continued to press him, and finally Akbar adopted an expedient which he anticipated would shame them out of further persistence. He announced that a great Mohammedan doctor was about to leap into a furnace with a Koran under his arm; and stated that he was confident that they would have no objection to following him with the Bible. The fathers, however, declined the test, fearing no doubt that the episode of Shadrach, Meshach, and Abednego was unlikely to be repeated.† Subsequently the friars obtained permission and returned to Goa, reaching that town in 1583. Twice subsequently Akbar requested Christian teachers, in 1591 and 1595, and expeditions were dispatched, only to meet with a like fate. Akbar was a seeker but he could not find. On the last occasion the missionaries went to Lahore, and accompanied

* Tennyson's *Akbar's Dream*.

† See Murray's *Discoveries and Travels in Asia*, vol. II, pp. 91, 92. The Mohammedan account of this debate in the " Akbernameh " tells the story of this challenge in a way that is, curiously enough, more disparaging to the Mohammedans. It asserts that the challenge came from the Christian side and was rejected by the Mohammedans with reproaches. See Elphinstone, *Hist. Ind.* Cowell's (ninth) edition, p. 523 note.

the prince into Cashmere; but soon returned, having accomplished nothing. And so ended, for the present, the attempts of the Portuguese to convert the Mogul Empire to Christianity. At few moments, perhaps, since Christianity was founded, has it had a greater opportunity; and seldom has it appeared to such disadvantage in comparison with another faith. During the boyhood of Akbar the fires of Smithfield were the concrete expression of that bigotry which he so detested; before he died he might have found another example nearer home in the Inquisition of Goa. In England men were burning their fellows; in India they were racking them; meantime Akbar was dreaming—dreaming dreams so profound that only Abu-l-Fazl and a few chosen spirits could interpret them. It was sublime, but it was many centuries too soon. His contemporaries did not understand him; and though some small portion of his mantle fell upon his successor, and reappeared in his great-grandson Dara, the populace eagerly returned to the idols of the market-place, and gave a cordial welcome to bigotry and persecution when revived by Aurangzib. But of all the thousands who came in contact with the lofty, though not wholly consistent, deism of the great philosopher and king, few were less qualified by nature and training cordially to sympathise with his searchings of heart than the missionary friars from Goa.

Portuguese Missionary Travellers

Before passing on to our next missionary traveller, it may be as well to add an illustration from Portuguese sources of Akbar's undeviating tolerance. Towards the close of his reign the Portuguese obtained a footing in Dacca, the great Bengal emporium. The Mohammedan mollahs there tried to alarm the people against them, warning them that Heaven would exact retribution if they allowed these "Kafirs," who purposely insulted the Prophet by eating pork and drinking wine, to dwell among them. The principal wife of the nabob was seriously alarmed by these predictions, and sought to get the strangers expelled. The case came before Akbar, and we can easily imagine the short shrift which he meted out to the bigoted religionists. In addition to forbidding all molestation of the Portuguese, he offered them the revenue of a certain amount of land as a gift.*

In his book of *Pilgrimes*, Samuel Purchas has a few pages devoted to Nicholas Pimenta, the Jesuit. He entitles them "Indian Observations, gathered out of the letters of Nicholas Pimenta, Visitor of the Jesuits in India, and of many others of that Societie, written from divers Indian regions, principally relating the countries and accidents of the Coast of Coromandel and of Pegu." Pimenta's letters were written in 1598, to Claudius Aquaviva, the Chief Jesuit, and relate the writer's visitation voyage from

* Murray, *Discoveries and Travels in Asia*, vol. II, p. 98.

Goa in December, 1597. Having reached Cochin, Pimenta dispatched thence two missions; one of these went to Bengal, the other to Pegu. After giving the substance of letters sent from Bengal by members of the Bengal mission, Pimenta describes the journey from St Thome. The account is valuable as containing some important information on the various kingdoms round the south and west coasts of Southern India. We hear of the King of Travancore, who was expecting an immediate attack from the King of Madura with 70,000 men. We hear too of the Naichus of Gingi, "who marvelled much that we chewed not the leaves of betel," the Naichus of Tanjore, and so on. These potentates were originally governors of provinces under the Empire of Vijayanagar, but on its humiliation in 1565 became independent. Perhaps the most interesting part of the letters is that in which he gives at length the extraordinary title which he alleges the existing representative of the old Rajah of Vijayanagar, who was then established at Chanderghirri, to have borne as a survival of the former greatness of the Emperor of "Narsinga." So curious a specimen of Oriental phraseology cannot be omitted; and in quoting it we may take leave of one who in spite of his brevity is yet one of the most interesting and valuable of all whom we may perhaps term minor travellers. The title runs as follows: "The husband of Subvast (that is) of Good Fortune, God of great provinces, King of the Greatest Kings and God of Kings, Lord of all Horse-forces, Master of those which know not how to Speake, Emperour of three Emperours, Conqueror of all which he seeth, and Keeper of all which he hath overcome, Dreadful to the eight coasts of the world, the Vanquisher of Muhametan Armies, Ruler of all provinces which he hath taken, Taker of the Spoiles and Riches of Ceilan, which far exceedeth the most Valiant man, which cut off the head of the Invincible, Virivalalam, Lord of the East, South, North, West, and of the Sea, Hunter of Elephants; which liveth and glorieth in Virtue Militarie."*

About 1612 Sebastian Manrique, a friar of the order of St Augustine, was sent to Bengal with three other missionaries to propagate Christianity in that province. During the course of the next thirteen years he travelled widely in India, and visited certain districts of which few accounts are extant. Starting presumably from Goa the four missionaries landed, after a voyage round the south of India, at "Angelim" (Ingelly), at the mouth of the western branch of the Ganges. Having been speedily brought into the presence of the local nabob, Musundulim, they were ordered to deliver up all the keys of the ship; but on the captain of the vessel intimating that they could not possibly

* *Purchas his Pilgrimes*, II, x, 1746.

comply, instructions were immediately issued for the execution of the speaker and Manrique. The two were seized, partially stripped, and bound, and were then hurried off to prison. The captain assured his companion in misfortune that this was only done in order to frighten them; but presently soldiers rushed in and began making furious flourishes round the victims' heads with naked scimitars, a diversion which they kept up for the greater part of the night. At last the captain was proved a true prophet, and a cry of friendship was raised and betel leaves presented; but not until Manrique had received a tremendous fright, which makes his statement that he was "perplexed and confused" easy of belief. On receiving permission to depart the friars started at once for Hugli.

At this point in his narrative* Manrique makes some valuable observations on the political and social condition of Bengal. He describes the great fertility of the Ganges plain, and the magnificence of its cotton fabrics. He asserts, however, that the prosperity of the country is seriously hampered by the oppressive nature of the rule of the Mogul representative in Bengal. If a land-holder cannot, for any reason whatever, pay his proper rent, the governor seizes not only his property but even his wife and children. The fault, however, we gather from

* The *Itinerario*, Rome, 1653.

Manrique, was not entirely on the side of the governor; the Bengali ryot made it a rule never to part with money without the application of the whip, while the necessity of this painful preliminary was strongly insisted upon by the ryot's wife, who, if she learnt that her lord has dispensed with it and paid without a struggle, put him on short rations for a time as a punishment. The people Manrique found to be a spiritless lot, who understood nothing better than rough treatment. Kindness was wasted on them. "He who gives blows is a master; he who gives none is a dog." Various remarks on the Hindu religion, especially on suttee, the natives' reverence for the Ganges and the cow, and their self-immolation at Jaggernat and Sagur, conclude Manrique's description of Bengal. His account of the devotees who sacrifice themselves at Sagur is very interesting. The island, he says, was at the time of his visit practically uninhabited, but was still the resort of pilgrims. The seas round it swarmed with crocodiles, and the fanatics threw themselves into the water in the hope of being devoured by them. Apparently, however, if the saurians refused the meal offered them, the would-be martyrs refused to accept the alternative chance of death by drowning, but came out of the water crying aloud that the god would not receive them as an offering on account of their sins. Gazing upon the pitiable spectacle, the missionary no doubt felt as did the poet* in after years, when the sight of so striking an example of the power of superstition wrung from him lines which were at once a prayer and a curse:

> On sea-girt Sagur's desert isle
> Mantled with thickets dark and dun,
> May never morn or starlight smile,
> Nor ever beam the summer sun.

Than Sagur, with all its "pomp of human sacrifice," no missionary could ask a stronger stimulus to exertion.

On leaving Bengal Manrique sailed for Chittagong, whence he proceeded to Arracan. After a prolonged stay here, he returned to Bengal, off which he was shipwrecked and taken prisoner; but on being liberated returned in safety to Goa. From Goa he set out for Malacca, and before leaving this part of the East Indies, visited Macao, the Philippines, and Cochin China. On returning, Manrique again made a lengthy stay in Bengal, and then proceeded up country to Agra, and thence to Lahore. His journey from Lahore down the Indus was one that was almost unique among the early travellers.

* John Leyden. A few more lines may perhaps be excused:

> Not all blue Ganga's mountain flood,
> That rolls so proudly round thy fane,
> Shall cleanse the tinge of human blood,
> Nor wash dark Sagur's impious stain.
> The sailor journeying on the main
> Shall view from far the dreary isle
> And curse the ruins of the pile
> Where mercy ever sued in vain.

Ten days brought him to Multan. His route took him through country abounding in large villages and excellent inns. At Multan the missionary arranged to go down the Indus with a merchant, who was conducting a commercial expedition to Tatta. Manrique here mentions the curious fact that the natives had a prejudice that a " Feringhi "* would ensure success to any undertaking in which he took part; hence he had no difficulty in obtaining permission to accompany them. Manrique's courage and resource in the subsequent adventures of the party makes us wonder whether their prejudice was not based on something more tangible and practical than superstition, for after passing Bhakkar they were attacked by two vessels and would have lost all their property had it not been for the shells which the militant missionary had prepared for such emergencies as these.† Wherever he went the people brought their sick to Manrique and continued to do so despite his protestations that he had no healing power. After their repulse of the pirates a considerable amount of desert country was passed through, but after passing Seivan the landscape improved, and finally Tatta was reached. At Tatta Manrique produced a " Firman " from the Mogul authorising the erection of a

* Europeans are, it is scarcely necessary to say, known as " Feringhis " in India.

† The presence of pirates on the Indus is significant of the disordered state of that part of the country under the successors of Akbar.

Christian church, which met with the utmost respect from the local governor. After seeing the foundations laid, he returned by land to Multan, passing Jesselmir on the way. From Multan Manrique travelled home to Europe by way of Cabul, Candahar, and Persia. So ended the travels of one whose wanderings comprised an extent of territory as wide as that of almost any traveller of whom we know, who time after time was involved in positions in which he was but "four or seven fingers' breadth removed from death," and may rightly be termed one of the most spirited and admirable figures among the many devoted and brave men whom the Roman Church gave to India in the early days of European contact with that country.

With Manrique we reach the last of the missionary friars whose narratives are at all useful. It is a little surprising that our investigations in this direction have not been more fruitful. Owing to the nature of their occupation the early missionaries not only visited places a little out of the common ruck, but were also compelled to mix familiarly with the people. In addition they were also men of at least a certain superficial education, and should have been able to observe with intelligence what they saw as well as record it with care and faithfulness. But not one of the records which contains the history of the travels of these clerics possesses more than minor value. The reason why the friars thus neglected their unrivalled opportunities is not clear. In modern times missionaries are our sources for a vast amount of ethnographical knowledge which we should not otherwise possess, and as compared with professed travellers provide no small proportion of the accessions to our insight into the ways of native races. The Portuguese missionaries of the sixteenth and seventeenth centuries who contribute to our knowledge are, on the other hand, when compared with others who visited India during their time, both few in number and insignificant in value.*

* No attempt has been made to deal comprehensively with the subject of Portuguese missions in India, only those missionaries whose travels possessed especial interest and value having received attention. The bulk of this chapter, with the exception of the pages dealing with Pimenta, has been adapted from Murray's *Discoveries and Travels in Asia.* Murray's authorities for this part of his subject were:—

Guzman, *Historia de las missiones che han becho los religiosos de la companbia de Jesus, para predicar el Santo Evangelio en la India Oriental y en los Reynos de Cbina y Japon.* Alcala, 1601.

Oriente Conquistado a Jesu Cbristo pelos Padres da companbia de Jesu da Provincia de Goa. 1710.

Cartas de la India. 1551, 1562, 1611.

Manrique, *Itinerario de las missiones del India Oriental.* Roma, 1653.

CHAPTER VI

The First Englishmen in India

Undying then should be our gratitude to the founders of the East India Company, for they were indeed the pioneers of the unparalleled colonial and mercantile prosperity of modern England, and we may be sure that wherever "The strong hearts of her sons" . . . are kept up by the high hopes on which they are perennially nourished in the invincible Republic of the West, and in the proud dominions of the British Crown in the great South Sea, there the names of those middle class Elisabethan merchant adventurers, who so well understood, when occasion called, how by transgressing, most truly to keep, the moral law, will be for ever cherished and revered, as of "brave men, and worthy patriots, dear to God, and famous to all ages."—*Sir George Birdwood.*

"THE sixteenth century witnessed the birth of the Mogul Empire; the seventeenth its prime maturity; the eighteenth its wretched and decrepit old age."* As a consequence of the outstanding position of that Empire during the hundred years which followed the death of Akbar, the history of seventeenth century India focusses itself upon that romantic personality whom the Western world knew as the "Great Mogul." The brilliance of Akbar's reign and his steady consolidation of almost the whole of Hindustan under a single rule had

* Mr S. Lane-Poole, in the *Quarterly Review*, vol. CLXXVI, p. 491.

slowly made his name known in Europe. Strange stories were told of his religious toleration and of the eager welcome which he accorded Christians at his court. But it was his reputed wealth which most attracted the attention of Elizabethan England. The scarcity of suitable investments for their savings in Europe,* and the prospect of a brilliant and lucrative return from commercial speculation in the East, led the merchants of England to turn their gaze toward India. Fresh, too, from their triumph over the Spanish Armada, the adventurous spirits of England were eager to seize for themselves that share of the trade which they may well have considered the legitimate fruit of their victory.† The prominence of the Empire over which the descendants of Tamerlane held sway decreed that, after a venture or two among the islands, the main stream of British commerce in India was to direct itself toward the land of the "Great Mogul."

But, long before the foundation of the East India Company, India had been visited by Englishmen. The first Englishman who is known to have visited the country was Thomas Stephens, who went to Goa in 1579, and became Rector of the Jesuits' College in Salsette. Before leaving England he studied at New College, Oxford. While in India he main-

* See Sir H. S. Maine's *International Law*, p. 205.

† Spain and Portugal were united in 1580.

tained a correspondence with his father, of which one or two letters are preserved by Purchas. These relate only to Goa and the district round, and possess no value from our present point of view. It is said that they roused great enthusiasm in England, and were one of the influences which led his countrymen to desire to trade directly with India.

Stephens was not a traveller. The first Englishman entitled to that appellation, as far as India is concerned, was "Master Ralph Fitch, Merchant of London," to use the title which Purchas gives him. With two other Englishmen, named Newbery and Leedes, he travelled to Ormuz, and thence crossed the Indian Ocean to Goa. In all Fitch was eight years away from England, starting his travels in 1583, and returning in 1591. On their way to Goa the three travellers visited Diu, which place Fitch tells us no vessels could pass without a permit from the Portuguese, and Chaul, where Fitch noticed some of the curious habits of the people. "They worship a cow," he says, "and esteem much of the cowe's dung to paint the walls of their houses. . . . They will kill nothing, not so much as a louse." The prevalence of suttee claimed his attention, as too did the custom of burning the dead. His remarks on this are curious. "They say if they should be buried, it were a great sinne, for of their bodies would come many wormes and other vermine, and when their bodies were consumed, these wormes would lack sustenance, which were a great sinne, therefore they will be burned." Purchas's brief annotation to this passage—" Mad reason for burning the dead "—is not without point.

On reaching Goa the three Englishmen were thrown into prison by the Portuguese governor on suspicion of being spies. After a time, and with considerable difficulty, they recovered their liberty, mainly through the good offices of Father Stephens, the English Jesuit mentioned above. In 1585 the three left Goa, and went to " Bisapor."* Fitch gives a quaint description of the idols here. " Some be like a cow, some like a Monkie, some like Buffles, some like Peacockes, and some like the Divell." The travellers then went on to Golconda, "the king whereof is called Cutup de lashac,"† and finally, after passing through various towns, including Burhanpur, they reached the "country of Zelabdim Echebar."‡ Fitch mentions the number of boy and girl marriages they saw celebrated on the way, and gives a description of them. Reaching Agra, which Fitch describes as a " very great citie and populous, built with stone, having fair and large streets with a faire river running by it," they did not stay there long, but pushed on to Fatepur, the residence of " the Great Mogor."

* Bijapur. † Mohammed Kuli. ‡ Akbar.

Fitch must have seen Akbar several times, as the three stayed in Fatepur till September, 1585, but very little is said about him in Purchas's version of his narrative. There are some remarks on the magnificence and style in which Akbar lived, and on the nature of the vehicles employed in the streets of Fatepur, and that is all.

At Fatepur the travellers parted. Newbery, according to Fitch, started for Lahore, to go thence overland to Persia, though Sir George Birdwood says he settled down as a shopkeeper at Goa.* Leede's entered Akbar's service as a jeweller; while Fitch set out on further peregrinations.

Sailing down the Jumna, Fitch started from Agra for Lower Bengal, passing Benares on the way. He gives a number of interesting remarks on the various rites and customs which he saw in the plain of the Ganges, but there is space for only one of them. It is a description of a Bengal marriage ceremony. "When they bee married the man and the woman come to the water side, and there is an old man which they call a Bramane, that is, a Priest, a Kow, and a Calfe, and a Kow with Calfe. Then the man and the woman, the Kow, and Calfe, and the old man, goe into the water together, and they give the old man a white cloth of foure yards long, and a basket crosse-bound with divers things in it:

* I do not know on what authority. See *Report on the Old Records*, p. 197.

the cloth he layeth upon the backe of the Kow, and then he taketh the Kow by the end of the tayle,* and sayeth certaine words: and shee hath a Copper or Brasse pot full of water, and the man doeth hold his hand by the old mans hand, and the wives hand by her husbands, and all have the Kow by the tayle, and they powre water out of the pot upon the Kowes tayle, and it runneth through all their hands, and they lade up water with their hands, and then the old man doeth tye him and her together by their clothes. Which done they goe round about the Kow and Calfe, and then they give somewhat to the poore which be alwaies there, and to the Bramane or Priest they give one Kow and Calfe, and afterward goe to divers of their Idols, and offer money, and lie downe flat upon the ground, and kisse it divers times, and then goe their way."†

Fitch then made his way to "Patenaw,"‡ where he noticed the migratory character of the people, who "like the Arabians have no certain abode."

After various travels in Bengal, in which he visited Satgaon, Hugli, and other places, and made a twenty-five days' journey into the "Country of Conche," "not far from Cochin China," Fitch went on a lengthly peri-

* Purchas has a characteristic note later on, when he finds this part of the cow in great demand for other purposes also. "Kow tayles in great request," he appends at the side of his narrative.

† *Purchas his Pilgrimes*, II, x, 1735.

‡ Patna.

grination to Pegu, Macao, Malacca, and Ceylon, at the end of which he doubled Cape Comorin, passed Quilon, and made Cochin in March, 1590.

He returned to Europe by Goa, Chaul, Ormuz, Busrah, Aleppo, and Tripoli, reaching London in April, 1591. Fitch's observations, as recorded in *Purchas his Pilgrimes*, are not of any especial value, and we can never forgive him for dismissing the great Akbar so curtly, and for failing to see that he was a far different personage from the numerous lordlings whom he met in his wanderings; but none the less he stands high among the famous travellers of England. Not only was he the first Englishman to emulate the experiences and adventures of the famous Portuguese and Italian travellers of former years, and the first to examine with his own eyes the commercial possibilities for Englishmen of the countries of the East, but the many difficulties which he overcame and the wide extent of ground which he covered make him a worthy predecessor of some of the better known English travellers of the seventeenth century.

While Fitch was in India, additional knowledge of that country and of its commercial possibilities had been gained by the energy of Sir Francis Drake. In 1587, Drake, who had sailed in the Indian Ocean ten years before, but had not touched India itself, captured a Portuguese carrack which was returning with a full cargo from Goa to Portugal. The examination of the *St Philip*, which was the first ship of the kind the English had taken, greatly opened the eyes of Englishmen as to the commodities to be obtained in the East, and conveyed to them besides a deal of other valuable information. This, combined with the letters of Father Stephens and the tale which Fitch had to tell, not to speak of the growing contempt for Portuguese and Spaniard which the defeat of the Armada had generated, determined Englishmen to establish direct commercial communication with India. Lancaster's expedition of 1591, and Dudley's of 1596,* were utter failures, all the ships being lost in each case; and for a time these disasters discouraged further enterprise.

In 1599 another English traveller left England for India. John Mildenhall, who, to judge from the Court Minutes of the East India Company,† served Richard Stapers, one of its first board of directors, in some fiduciary capacity, started in this year on an overland journey to India. His object was to try to negotiate with the "Great Mogul" some kind of

* The captain was Benjamin Wood.

† "Letter received from John Mednoll to his master, Rich. Stapers, declaring what privileges he had obtained in the Indies, and offering them and his service to the Company for £1,500 in hand." Court Minutes, 1608, June 21.

commercial treaty or arrangement, which should be a basis for the English trade which was so soon to commence there. He went by sea to Aleppo, and travelled overland through Armenia, Kurdistan, Persia, and Afghanistan, and finally, after passing through Candahar and Lahore, reached Agra in 1603. On the third day after his arrival Mildenhall was admitted to the presence of Akbar, and made him a present of twenty-nine horses and some jewels, much to that potentate's delight. On a second audience being granted he stated his requests; they were, firstly, friendship between Akbar and the Queen of England, secondly, permission for the English to trade in his dominions, and lastly, his neutrality in the event of English and Portuguese ships fighting in his seas. "His greatness," said Mildenhall to the king, "and renowned kindness unto Christians was so much blased throughout the world, that it had come into the furthermost parts of the Westerne Ocean."* Akbar ordered these requests to be put in writing, and promised a speedy answer. In the meantime he set to work to ascertain particulars of the power and character of the nation to which his new visitor belonged. On inquiring of some Portuguese Jesuits,† who

* "Letter of John Mildenhall to M. Richard Staper, written from Casbin in Persia, the third day of October, 1606." *Purchas his Pilgrimes*, 1, iii, 115.

†Possibly those of the expedition of 1595 mentioned in the preceding chapter.

were at his court, he received the unpromising assurance that the English were "a complete nation of thieves," and that Mildenhall's visit was a preliminary to an attempt to wrest from him some of his chief ports. After this, the king and his council, were, as Mildenhall puts it, "flat against" him; but this antagonism was only made known to Mildenhall by private intelligence, and was not betrayed by the demeanour of the king. He even promised the envoy that he was willing to accede to all his demands except that which asked for freedom to fight the Portuguese in his dominions. To this request, however, Mildenhall obstinately adhered, and received from the king an assurance that he would reconsider the point. Nothing accrued, and Mildenhall ceased attending the Emperor's court; but resumed attendance on Akbar complaining of his absence. Soon, however, he grew weary of lingering in this aimless fashion; and his troubles were increased by the fact that all the influential men whom he might have bribed with a view to the gaining of his wishes had already been over-bribed by the Jesuits. To add to his misfortunes, Jesuit machination caused his interpreter to desert him, and he was compelled to spend six months in learning Persian. As soon as he could speak it "something reasonably," he went "in great discontentment" to the king, and told him outright "how small it would stand with so great a prince as his majesty had report to be, to delay me so many years only upon the report of two Jesuites." Akbar's answer was that he would arrange a public audience, in which each of the two European disputants might plead his own cause. Mildenhall stated his wrongs, and dwelt particularly on the insolence of the Jesuits in calling the English thieves; adding that, were it not for the sacred character of their calling, he would inflict corporal vengeance on them. In the event Mildenhall, by conclusively proving that the hostility of the Jesuits to the English was preventing the king from receiving frequent presents from the Queen of England, completely turned the tables upon his reverend antagonists, in a way which made the monarch "very merrie"; with the result that thirty days later he was able to leave with all his demands granted, and a document signed and sealed to that effect, "to my own great contentment, and as I hope to the profit of my nation." He returned through Persia to Kasbin,* whence he sent news home.†

* Kasbin is north west of Teheran, some seventy miles from the southern shore of the Caspian Sea.

† Mildenhall comes frequently into the later history of the East India Company. The following extracts from the Calendar of State Papers (Colonial), 1513–1616, will give some idea of his later career, which can scarcely be called creditable :

May 30, 1609. Committee to confer with John Midnall concerning his demands, and project for going to "Mawgoule" in the East Indies.

July 27, 1609. Petition of John Midnall to the King, declaring his ten years' travel and charge of 3,000 (*sic*) in the discovery of a rich

Mildenhall's hope that his "treaty" would be for the benefit of his nation was not fulfilled, and it made no difference to the subsequent transactions between the English and the "Great Mogul." How far we can accept the envoy's story of his "treaty" is doubtful. It is almost certain that he did not obtain any sort of treaty in the usual sense of the term. Akbar was an enlightened king, but he possessed to the full the Oriental sense of dignity. What four years' negotiation on the part of Hawkins and Roe did not obtain it is very improbable that Mildenhall obtained in half that time. It is possible that he obtained some sort of a local "firman," which naturally became waste paper on the death of Akbar; but this hardly harmonises with Mildenhall's account. Whether the envoy was duped, whether he deliberately tried to cover his failure with the story of a fictitious treaty, or whether Akbar's greatness appeared in this transaction

trade in the dominions of the Great Mogul, and praying that he and his coadventurers may be permitted to enjoy the privileges he had obtained there.

Oct. 20, 1609. . . . John Midnall . . . nominated for factors.

Nov. 17, 1609. Committee to confer with John Midnall concerning his demands to be employed.

Nov. 18. 1609. Mr Mildnall not thought fit to be engaged.

Aug. 19, 1614. Newman employed by Mr Stapers, Abbott, and others, to recover goods from John Midnall who died at the king's court at Adsmere (Ajmere). There is some hope of getting the goods.

Sept. 20, 1614. Goods and money to the value of 9,000 dollars recovered from John Midnall, who had fled from Persia to the Indies. He left his goods to his two bastard children in Persia by an Indian woman, and a Frenchman for his executor. . . . The property amounted to about £500, being the proceeds of goods sold by Midnall at 50 per cent. loss.

as in all else, and some real arrangement was made, are questions it is impossible to decide.

As for his account of his experiences, it is mainly personal in character, and sheds but little light on the political or social condition of the country. A few sidelights on Mogul Court life are obtainable from it, such as the universal practice of present-giving, which was *de rigueur* there, and was such a drain on the resources of ambassadors under Akbar's successor; but for this later writers are a better authority.

With Mildenhall we reach the last of the three pioneers of British intercourse with India. Like the Portuguese missionaries, they are of comparatively insignificant value to us as sources of knowledge. Two other nations were destined to struggle with England for the prize which was slipping from the grasp of Portugal. Among the pioneers of the one was Huyghen van Linschoten; among those of the other was Francois Pyrard de Laval. Both of these men wrote works which stand in the very first rank of those which enabled their contemporaries to gain some idea of the country which they had visited. But the pioneers of the nation which was destined ultimately to oust all others from the prize, toward which so many hands were stretched to grasp, cared so little for the philosophic aspect of the country in which they travelled that they gave to their eager countrymen nothing but a few brief letters and a barren and gossipy journal.*

* It is thought that a short chronological table of relevant events between Stephens's voyage to Goa and the Embassy of Hawkins may be found useful.

1579. Father Thomas Stephens goes to India.
1583. Fitch, Newbery and Leedes start for India. Linschoten at Goa.
1586. Sir Thomas Cavendish sails round the world.
1587. Drake captures the *St Philip.*
1588. Defeat of the "Spanish Armada."
1591. Private mercantile expedition under James Lancaster. All ships lost.
1592. Capture of Port. carrack *Madre de Dios.* Valuable information *re* Indian trade gained.
1595. Cornelius Houtman's fleet sails to Sumatra.
1596. Private venture of Sir Robert Dudley's three ships under Capt. B. Wood. Never heard of again.
1599. Dutch raise price of pepper against English. Meeting at "Founder's Hall." Company formed. Mildenhall starts for Agra.
1600. Company receives Royal Charter.
1602. Dutch East India Company formed out of number of small companies. "First Voyage" of English Company under J. Lancaster to Achin and Sumatra.
1604. Michelborne trades with private licence. "Second Voyage," under Sir H. Middleton (to Amboina).
1606. "Third Voyage," under Keelinge, Hawkins, and D. Middleton. Embassy of Hawkins.

CHAPTER VII

Linschoten—Pyrard de Laval—Pietro della Valle

Non tulit hinc secum Piper, Aurum, Balsama, Gemmas,
Costum, Aloen, Myrrham, Cinnama, Thura, Crocum.
Rettulit hic Mores Hominesque Viator et Urbes,
Regna, habitus, linguas, prœlia, jura, deos.
—*Ar. Jonstonus. Med. Reg.*

AT the close of the last chapter the names of two famous travellers were mentioned. One of these was a Dutchman whose account of his travels exerted such an influence upon his countrymen that he may rightly be called the originator of Dutch commerce with India; the other was a Frenchman who was a prominent member of what was practically the first French commercial enterprise in the East.* In the case of each of these two men the extent of their travels in India proper was comparatively trifling, and out of all proportion to the value of the books they wrote. A similar disproportion is the characteristic of yet a third traveller of this period, Pietro della Valle, an Italian. To the travels of these three men, whose visits to India each fell within the forty years that witnessed the establishment of the various

* But see page 123, below.

rival European trading companies, the present chapter will be devoted.

The first Dutch enterprise which successfully reached the East Indies was that of Cornelius Houtman in 1595; but this was only rendered possible by John Huyghen van Linschoten, who visited Portuguese India in 1583. Linschoten, who was a native of the province of Utrect, went at the age of sixteen to Seville in Spain, and in April, 1583, sailed for Goa in the suite of Vincente de Fonseca, who had been appointed to the Archbishopric of Goa. Soon after his arrival at Goa Linschoten saw Fitch, Newbery, and Leedes arrested as spies; and, subsequently, united with Father Stephens and others in procuring their release. After he had been at Goa five years, Linschoten was thrown out of employment by the death of the Archbishop; and having no reason for remaining in India decided to return to Europe. In January, 1589, he set sail from Cochin. The fleet on its way home touched at St Helena to take in provisions, and here Linschoten met Gerrit van Afhausen, a native of Antwerp, who had made a voyage to Malacca, and obtained from him a good deal of information relative to sea routes which he later inserted in his book.* After touching at Ascension and the Azores, the fleet reached Tercera, where Linschoten and Afhausen disembarked,

* *Voyages into ye Easte and Weste Indies*, Dutch Original, 1596. English Translation, 1598.

and made a prolonged stay. It was 1592 before Linschoten reached Lisbon, whence he made his way to Holland in September of that year. In 1596 he published an account of his investigations and discoveries, though no doubt the valuable information which he had gathered with regard to the trade routes and the state of the Portuguese power and commerce in the East Indies was communicated to the leaders of Dutch commercial enterprise long before the publication of the book.

The book at once created a sensation, and was translated into several languages. It is valuable chiefly as a picture of the Portuguese Empire in India at the beginning of its decadence. The startling exposure of its weakness and of the corruption and immorality of its administrators immensely stimulated not only the Dutch but all Europe in its desire to endeavour to wrest some of the profits of the Indian trade from the hands of those who had monopolised them for nearly a century. The route from Europe to Cochin was clearly explained, and other routes, such as those to China, Japan, and the Archipelago, on which Linschoten had taken pains to gather information, were more or less carefully detailed. To the fact that Holland's pioneer in the matter of the commercial possibilities of India was Linschoten, who went to India by the Cape route, while that of England was Fitch, who used the Ormuz route, is partly due the early priority which the Hollanders won over the English in the days of the struggle for the Indian trade which began so soon after Linschoten's return to Europe.

Linschoten, as has been made clear, was not a great traveller, as far as the actual extent of the ground he covered is concerned. It has been shown that he did not venture beyond the Portuguese settlements. His book is, however, full of valuable remarks on almost all the countries comprised in the Portuguese sphere of influence, extending from Cambay on the one side to Singapore, China, and Japan on the other. Linschoten's information on these places does not of course possess the value of first-hand evidence, though his authority was doubtless good in the main. A few remarks which were probably based on personal observation call for attention. They relate to the Malabar coast, parts of which there is no doubt he visited.

Linschoten tells us, as we knew already from the narratives of Conti, Abd-er-Razzak, and other early travellers, that Calicut was formerly the most famous town in all Malabar, and, he even adds, in all India; and then proceeds to tell us of the degeneration into which it had fallen. "It was the chief towne," he says, "of Malabar where the Samoriin, which is the Emperor, holdeth his Court, but because the

Portingalles at their first coming and discovery of India were oftentimes deceyved by him, they resorted to the King of Cochin, who (as then) was subject to the Samoriin, being of small power. But when the Portingals began to Prosper and to get possession in the country, and so become maisters of the sea, Calecut beganne to decay, and to lose both name and traffique, and now at this time it is one of the townes of least account in all Malabar, and Cochin to the contrarie, their king being very rich and richer than the Samoriin. . . ."* Apparently when the Portuguese first reached India, the Malabar coast comprised a series of independent or semi-independent states, overshadowed both by the power of Vijayanagar and by the wealthy city of Calicut. In Linschoten's time the situation was still the same save that the power of the Hindu kingdom was broken, while Cochin and not Calicut was now " primus inter pares." Linschoten quotes a story of a certain Ceruman Perumal, a king of Malabar, who in 350 A.D., he alleges, departed on a pilgrimage, dividing up his kingdom among Cochin, Cannanore, Quilon, and other towns, but leaving Calicut supreme. So, says Linschoten, they have remained to this day, save that Cochin is exalted at the expense of Calicut. Other remarks follow on Ceylon and the Cingalese, the Coromandel

* p. 68 of the Hak. Soc. Edition of Linschoten's travels, the text of which is the old English translation of 1598.

Coast, "Narsinga," Bengal and the River Ganges, Pegu, Siam, the islands, China, and Japan. In these we need not accompany the author, as, for all of those districts which are in India proper, the amount of first-hand material is sufficiently large to enable us to dispense with all other.

In 1601, some citizens of St Malo, Laval, and Vitrè, eager to emulate the Dutch, formed a company and equipped two vessels for the Indian trade. Except for the voyage of Jean Parmentier of Dieppe in 1529 to Sumatra, this expedition of 1601 was the first enterprise of the French in East Indian waters. There were two vessels, the *Croissant* and the *Corbin.* François Martin, a native of Vitré, who was in the *Croissant*, wrote an account of the voyage of that vessel which has since almost disappeared.* On the *Corbin* was a native of Laval, whose account of the voyage of the ship and its disastrous outcome has become famous. His name was Francois Pyrard and later generations have always known him as François Pyrard de Laval.

The ships sailed on May 18, 1601. Having touched at St Helena in November, the expedition rounded the Cape of Good Hope three days after Christmas. Terrible scurvy then broke out among the crews, and many deaths ensued. On July 1 the *Corbin* was wrecked on

* There were two editions, 1604 and 1609.

the Maldives, and the castaways were thrown upon the islands in a semi-starved condition.* Twelve men stole a boat and succeeded in making Quilon, only to be immediately consigned to the galleys of the Portuguese. Six weeks after the wreck the captain died. In the end four alone remained of the forty who had been thrown on the islands. Among them was Pyrard de Laval.

The castaways had, in the meantime, been made captive by the natives, but, save for the loss of their liberty, were not inhumanely treated. Pyrard came off best of all. He studied the Maldive language and social institutions, and gathered the store of facts which he afterwards embodied in the first volume of his book,† which remains an authority on the Maldives to this day. In February, 1607, after the Frenchmen had endured over four years' captivity, an expedition, attracted by the hope of obtaining the *Corbin's* cannon, arrived at Malé from Chittagong, which, after attacking and killing the native sultan, seized Pyrard and his companions, and carried them to Chittagong. On their arrival there, the

* The fate of the *Croissant* was more delayed, but almost equally disastrous. It reached Achin, July 24, 1602, and left November 20 of the same year. Rounding the Cape after a terrible storm, it reached St Helena March 3. Off Cape Finisterre the ship foundered, but not before the famished crew and part of the cargo had been taken on board by three Flemish ships coming from Venice. See Martin, *Description du premier voyage faict aux Indes Orientales par les François.*

† *Voyage de François Pyrard de Laval*, etc. Paris, 1619.

local Rajah placed no restrictions upon their freedom, and after expressing a wish that they should remain with him, acceded to their request to be allowed to depart, and gave them passage in a ship bound for Calicut. After three weeks' voyage, Pyrard and the other Frenchmen landed at Muttingals, a port of the Malabar pirates between Cannanore and Calicut; and on journeying to the latter town by land, he was received with immense enthusiasm on announcing that he was an enemy of the Portuguese. Pyrard's narrative here becomes very valuable as shedding light on the attitude of the Samorin and the Portuguese toward the pirates of Malabar. From this and other sources we gather that the Samorin and the pirates were in a secret alliance, which enabled both to snap their fingers, to a certain degree, at the hostility of the Portuguese.

At Calicut the Frenchmen stayed eight months. At the end of that period two Jesuits persuaded three of them to leave Calicut with letters of safe-conduct to Cochin; but they were immediately seized and cast into the "Tronco" at Cochin. The horrors of this dungeon, according to Pyrard's description, almost baffle belief, and are a confirmation of what we have gathered from Pinto and others of the subject of Portuguese cruelty in India. After nine days of this torture, the Frenchmen were released, and shipped to Goa, where Pyrard spent some time both in the hospital and in the prison. He gives a caustic account of the moral laxity, stupid pride, and widespread gambling, which characterised the decaying power of Portugal, and was especially exemplified at Goa. On leaving Goa, Pyrard visited Ceylon, in which island he remarks the constant conflicts of the Portuguese and the natives, and the Malaccas. Early in 1610 Pyrard returned home from Goa by the Cape route, and after touching at Brazil on his way finally reached Laval in February, 1611.

It is not possible to do adequate justice to Pyrard de Laval by mere quotation; in addition to which the nature of his information, as far as the bulk is concerned, is such as not to demand extended notice in the present work. The Maldives, the description of which is Pyrard's greatest title to fame, fall outside the scope of the present essay; and information on the condition of the Portuguese settlements is scarcely directly within it, as the work is concerned more especially with the native governments. In that part, moreover, of his narrative where he becomes directly relevant to the present subject he is, owing to the localities to which he confined his travels, able only to amplify knowledge which we already possess. Some of these amplifications* are interesting and perhaps deserving

* e.g., Pyrard, in opposition to most other travellers, says the Nairs, and not the common folk, uttered the warning cry of "Popo." He also explains the system of Nair "escorts" (see above, p. 70). "For a party of twenty," he says, "one Nair suffices" (p. 359, Hak. Soc. Ed.)

of mention, but it seems scarcely worth while, for the sake of a few minute additions, to re-survey ground which has already received ample attention. With these few remarks, therefore, we may perhaps be allowed to take leave of a traveller whose combination of romantic adventure with perspicacity of observation render him one of the most striking figures in all our lengthly list.

We come, lastly, to Pietro della Valle, the famous Italian traveller. Though his actual Indian travels were not wide, and consequently do not demand very detailed attention, his name is one of the best known among all the early European visitors to India. Appreciation of the value of his observations in Turkey and Persia has always been freely accorded him. Praise from Southey no one need despise, and della Valle's book obtained it; but the crowning distinction of a flattering reference to his work by one of the greatest of the world's historians would have been sufficient compensation had all others neglected him.* But the record of his Indian travels, limited though they were in extent, and confined, too, to districts of which the greater part had been visited by previous travellers, is not less valuable. It amplifies our knowledge in that peculiar way which is open only to an observant mind trained by experience

* Southey calls him "that excellent traveller." "No traveller," says Gibbon, "knew or described Persia so well as Pietro della Valle."

and equipped with a copious store of general information. Pietro della Valle came to India spurred solely by the desire for knowledge. Speaking of such travellers as these, in whose voyagings desire for profit has been no incentive, Sir Henry Yule remarks that "the Prince of all such is Pietro della Valle, the most insatiate in curiosity, the most intelligent in apprehension, the fullest and most accurate in description."*

Born at Rome in 1586, Pietro della Valle, after seeing a certain amount of military service, joined, in 1611, a Spanish fleet on an expedition to Barbary. Owing to a disappointment in love, he left and went to Naples, and, assuming the habit of a pilgrim, gained the sobriquet of "Pellegrino." He began his travels proper in 1614. In that year he embarked for Constantinople in a Venetian ship, and in the following year travelled in Asia Minor, Egypt, and Palestine. At Baghdad he met and married an Assyrian Christian, who accompanied him in his travels through Persia, but, to Della Valle's great grief, died near the Gulf of Ormuz. The bereaved husband caused the remains to be coffined, and carried them with him in all his subsequent travels, until he finally returned to Rome. At Bander Ser he tried to embark for India, but found it difficult owing to the fact that the English and Persians were besieging

* *Diary of Sir W. Hedges*, Hak. Soc. Edition, vol. II, p. 343.

the Portuguese in Ormuz. An attempt, however, from Lar was more successful, and the traveller reached Surat in February, 1623.

On reaching Surat Pietro della Valle immediately came in contact with Mogul rule. At the hands of subsequent travellers the Surat "Customers" (so they termed the Custom House officials) often receive severe criticism; but della Valle does not seem to have suffered more than the usual inconvenience familiar to all who have ever passed from one country to another. His account of his experiences would not read very strangely if written in connection with many a modern "douane." "Near the place," he says, "where the boats land stands the Dogana, or Custom House, and it took us some time to dispatch there, because they observe narrowly all goods that are brought in, . . . nor will they suffer strangers to enter till they be first known, and have licence, as 'tis also practiced in Venice. In all this they proceed with so great wariness and good order, that it being known that I conducted with me the Signora Mariuccia, altho' a girl very young, the Capo or President of the Dogana required likewise to be informed of her quality."*

Pietro della Valle remarks the presence of the Dutch in Surat, and dilates on the absolute freedom of religion extended to all in Guzerat.

* From the Hak. Soc. Translation and Edition of *Pietro della Valle's Travels.*

"The Gran Moghel" he states, "makes no difference in his dominions between the one sort and the other." He next mentions the prevalence of Hindu boy and girl marriages, of idol-worship, and of slavery. He tells us that the Hindu women go about "with their faces uncovered, and can be freely seen by every one both at home and abroad," a remark which is instructive in view of the change of manners which has since taken place in this respect. The discovery of some large artificial pools outside Surat leads the traveller to enter upon a short discussion of the frequent occurrence of reservoirs in India.

While at Surat della Valle heard several rumours of the events which were taking place in the Mogul kingdom owing to the ambition of Khurram, one of Jehangir's sons. This leads him to enter upon a long sketch, in which we need not follow him, of the previous history of the Mogul rulers of Hindustan. It is both accurate and informing. It is from della Valle, among others, that we hear that the unfortunate Khursu, Jehangir's eldest son, only had his eyes "sewn up,"* and not put out, by his father's orders.

On leaving Surat, della Valle went to Cambay. Here, of course, like all others, he noticed the remarkable reverence for animal life that prevailed. He visited a "Hospital of Birds,"

* This probably means that a bandage was sewn round the head so that the eyes were blindfolded.

where he saw some lame, sick, and mateless birds and some tiny orphan mice. "A venerable Old Man with a white beard," he says, was "keeping them in a box amongst Cotton," and tending them diligently, "with his spectacles on his nose, giving them milk to eat with a bird's feather, because they were so little that as yet they could eat nothing else; and, as he told us, he intended when they were grown up to let them go free whither they pleased."

Della Valle next enters upon a dissertation on caste and morality among the Hindus. He asserts that there were eighty-four sects or parties of men in India "known and distinguished by descent or pedigree." They never, he says, rise or fall, or change their condition. A Banian (or Factor) is always a factor; a Rajput (or Soldier) is always a soldier. In connection with caste he mentions a curious drinking custom designed to avoid contamination. Various people were enabled to drink from the same vessel on a journey by holding it high above the mouth and gulping down the stream of liquid that was poured out above, without even touching the vessel with their lips. Della Valle's testimony to the morality of the Hindus at this period is glowing, and contrasts with that of other writers.* Adultery, fornication, and unnatural offences were, he tells us, considered great crimes. Adultery in the other party was

* e.g. *Mœurs des Peuples de l'Inde* (Dubois).

the sole cause of divorce, and polygamy was rare, though practised. The traveller takes occasion to point out the inconvenience of the law forbidding the remarriage of widows. Suttee,* to judge from della Valle's statement that he had not so far† seen an actual example, seems to have been decreased by the Mogul discouragement of the rite. The attitude of the Mohammedan sovereigns of India toward the practice of suttee may be described as permissive under protest. They did not actually forbid it, but required the would-be devotee to obtain a licence from the governor of her district, who never gave it till he had examined the woman with the utmost strictness to see that it was of her own free will that she was sacrificing herself. It is to this policy that della Valle attributes the scarcity of suttees near Surat and Cambay.

Ahmedabad was the next place that della Valle visited. Here he remarked two pulpits "handsomely built of stone, . . . where 'tis the Custome to read the King's Commandments publicly." We learn that Ahmedabad shared with Agra, Mandu, and Lahore the privilege of being the seat of the Great Mogul's Palace and Court. On attempting to leave Ahmedabad for Cambay, della Valle was inconvenienced by a proclamation which had been made in the

* It is interesting to notice that between 1815 and 1828 there were 8,134 instances of suttee in British India. It was forbidden in 1829.

† It should be remembered that della Valle had as yet only visited Surat and Cambay, and his generalisations apply to this district only.

town, owing to the "new Commotion between the Moghol and his son, Sultan Chorrom,"* to the effect that "no souldiers' Wives nor other persons of quality should go out of the city by land." As della Valle was accompanied in all his travels by the Syrian Mariuccia, a persuasive petition backed by a more persuasive present was necessary before the governor would grant them permission to leave.

Next we have an interesting social sidelight: "Coming from Nagra (Nagar) I saw some naked and besmeared Men, who were of a Race of Indians accounted by themselves the most sordid and Vile Race of all in India, because they eat everything, even the uncleanest animals, as Rats and the like, whence they are called in Persian Habal-Chor, which signifies a Man that accounts it lawful to eat anything. The Indians call them Der" (better Dher or Dhed), "and all people in general abhor not only to converse with, but even to touch them. They are all sufficiently poor, and live for the most part by begging, or exercising the most sordid trades in the Commonwealth, which others disdain to meddle with." It should be remembered that these "most sordid trades" are absolutely necessary to the health of the community.

Having returned to Cambay, della Valle travelled down the coast to Goa. He mentions the danger from attack by the Malabar pirates,

* i.e., Khurram.

which made it too risky to go by sea. The audacity and strength of these scourges of the Indian trade, of whom we hear continually in the pages of almost all of our travellers, is exemplified by the fact of their coming so far north. The traveller now delays his narrative of his observations to give a careful account of the three "Reguli" of the Deccan, the Nizam Shah, the Kutb Shah, and the Adil Shah. Proceeding southward by Honavar, "Pangi," and "Garsopa," della Valle reached Ikkeri. On his way there he saw some little boys being taught Arithmetic in the Sand in curious fashion without paper or writing instrument of any kind.* At Ikkeri he saw a native funeral. The corpse was carried sitting in a chair, tied to prevent it falling, and clothed in ordinary attire as if alive. The seat was covered behind and on the side with red and other colours. The dead person could be seen only from the front, where the chair was open. The corpse was in this condition placed on the funeral pile. Della Valle ascertained that the custom was similar in the case of those who were buried. Not long after della Valle was at the same time shocked and delighted to meet a suttee who was about to immolate herself. When he vainly tried to dissuade her, she argued the matter out calmly and dispassionately, and finished by asking him to contribute

* A similar method of education, in which palm-leaves were used, is, or was till recently, practised in India. See Monier-Williams, *Modern India*, Ed. of 1879, p. 220.

something toward the fuel. His scruples would not allow him to do this, but instead he assured her that he would do his best to immortalise her. In pursuance of his promise he tells us that the lady's name was Giaccoma.

On leaving Ikkeri, highly rejoiced, save for his pity for the victim, to have witnessed a suttee, and bearing with him a Canarese book presented him there, della Valle made his way to Barselore, which he describes. Passing through Mangalore and Banghel, he finally reached Olala, the limit of his travels in India, which at the time of his visit owned the sway of a queen, who, from his account, seems to have been decidedly primitive.

She was, he says, as black as an Ethiopian, and always went about alone on foot, save for an escort of six foot-soldiers. A cloak round the head and some thick pieces of white cotton cloth round the waist were the sum total of the royal attire. As della Valle quaintly remarks, she was "like a dirty kitchen wench more than a queen."

He obtained an audience with this potentate, and had an interesting talk with her. Some gossipy details of Olala and of its relations with the neighbouring state of Banghel are given. In these little principalities, which seem to have been examples of the numerous semi-independent states on or near the Malabar coast, the Calicut law of inheritance is stated to have prevailed. From Olala, Pietro della Valle returned to Mangalore, from which port he went by ship to Calicut, being threatened on the way by pirates. Of this town, which, despite its decline, due to Portuguese hostility, was still important, he appends a full description, which, however, contains but few facts which we have not learnt from other sources. He visited the Samorin's palace, and saw there all that was to be seen, including the King himself and two young princesses. At the close of 1623 della Valle left Calicut by sea, and after a strenuous fight with pirates and visits to one or two coast towns, reached Goa. At the close of 1624 he began his return home to Europe. From Goa he went by sea to Muscat, and travelled thence by Busrah, Aleppo, and Naples to Rome, which he reached in 1626.

On reaching Rome Pietro della Valle performed a duty which he had kept continually before his eyes during four years of travel—that of giving his dead wife burial in Italian soil. The Italian's romantic fidelity to his Armenian wife inspired some lines* which, with a pretty

* They are printed in the Hak. Soc. Edition of these Travels, and run as follows :

"Aeneadum suboles! Albani sanguinis heros!
Aeneae proavi quam bene facta refers.
Ille senem ex Asia fertur vexisse parentem;
Ex Asia conjux est tibi ducta comes.
Par utrique fides esset, nisi quod tua major
Est pietas, Italum gloria Valliade.
Ille senem extinctum Sicula tellure reliquit;
Tu Romam extinctae conjugis ossa vehis."

and pleasing conceit, compared his action to that of a more famous if more mythical traveller than della Valle. The parallel which they draw between the deed of the latter-day Italian and that of the filial founder of the race of his Roman ancestors is not by any means devoid of point. His act of devotion completed, Pietro della Valle felt himself free to let his fancy wander. It perhaps a little spoils the poetry of della Valle's devotion, but it was not an unfitting termination to his Eastern travels that for his second wife he should have taken the lady who had accompanied him during almost their whole course, in attendance, first on his Armenian wife, and then on her corpse.

From one point of view there is nothing that gives us such an insight into the comparatively high state of civilisation in India during the medieval period as the immunity with which strangers from a foreign country were able to take their womenfolk with them on their travels in India. In the fifteenth century we saw Conti doing so with perfect safety; at the beginning of the seventeenth Pietro della Valle supplies us with a second example. Had the positions been reversed, and an Indian traveller attempted to travel with his family through any of the more civilised countries of Europe between the beginning of the fifteenth and the close of the sixteenth century, it is doubtful whether the treatment he would have received would have been in any way comparable to that which the natives of India, Hindu and Mohammedan alike, meted out to their " Feringhi " visitors.

CHAPTER VIII

English Ambassadors at the Court of Jahangir

"Our true and undoubted Attorney, Procurator, Legate, and Ambassador" to that "high and mighty Monarch, the Greate Mogoar, King of the Orientall Indyes, of Condahy, of Chismer, and of Corason."—*From Sir Thomas Roe's Commission.**

IN a previous chapter it has been related how Sir John Mildenhall went on a journey to the Court of Akbar, with a view to the arrangement of a commercial treaty. In the reign of James I two Englishmen were sent out to his successor Jahangir upon a similar errand. One of these was William Hawkins, the sailor; the second Sir Thomas Roe, the diplomat. Both were ambassadors in the sense that they were the representatives of the King of England at a foreign Court; but the commission of Roe was far more formal than that of his predecessor. The journals of both men are of the highest interest.

Akbar died in 1605, and Selim ascended the vacant throne with the title of Jahangir, or World-Grasper. In 1606 the East India Company undertook what is known as their "third voyage," the first which had any dealings with

* See Mr S. Lane-Poole's *Medieval India*, p. 306.

the Mogul dominions. The expedition consisted of three ships. In command of one was Keelinge, of another David Middleton, of the third William Hawkins. Hawkins sailed straight to Surat, and landed, leaving his ship with orders to go on to Bantam.* Before leaving for Agra he suffered a good deal from the hostility of the Portuguese and the rapacity of the local Mogul authorities, who pillaged his goods, only paying such a price, Hawkins tells us, as their "own barbarous conscience afforded." In February, 1609, the sailor left Surat, and after many narrow escapes from assassination by the way, arrived at Agra in April. He began at once to look for lodgings "in a very secret manner," upon hearing of which the Mogul sent troops of horse to search for him in all directions. He was speedily introduced into Jahangir's presence, and gave him the letter from King James which he had brought with him. Jahangir accepted it, and employed a Jesuit to read it to him; but before doing so assured Hawkins that he would grant every request which it contained; a worthless piece of Oriental courtesy which it is to be hoped the sailor knew how to estimate at its proper worth.

Subsequently, on ascertaining that Hawkins spoke Turkish,† a language with which he also

* It was captured by the Portuguese on the way.

† "Perceiving I had the Turkish tongue, which himself well understood...." Such is Hawkins' narrative, as given in *Purchas his Pilgrimes*, I, iii, 210. What Jahangir spoke was not Constantinopolitan Turkish,

was acquainted, Jahangir invited him to a private audience. Hawkins made the most of his opportunity, and complained of the wrongs which the English suffered from the Portuguese, as well as of the high-handed action towards himself of Mukarrab Khan, the Governor of Surat. The Mogul assured him that he should receive full restitution, and that he would satisfy him as regarded the Portuguese. Hawkins also requested permission to go to Surat to establish an English factory there; and, in addition, asked for full freedom from all restrictions on trade. But Jahangir was not inclined to part so soon with his interesting visitor, and, by way of inducing him to stay, offered him an appointment of 400 horse, with a yearly allowance equal to £3,200, together with the honourable title of "Khan." Hawkins did not hesitate to accept; he felt that he could benefit the company's trade more by remaining near Jahangir than by going to Surat, and, as he added with refreshing candour, "in the meantime I should feather my own nest."

The "Inglis Khan" was now in high favour, and it was no wonder that "the Portugals were like madde dogges." Hawkins evidently suited

but Turki; and though the two are by no means identical, sufficient resemblance exists between them to make it probable that Jahangir had little more trouble in understanding Hawkins than two provincials from widely-sundered parts of England have in grasping each other's meaning. I am informed that the Turkish spoken at Constantinople is readily understood by the Turcomans of Central Asia, and that Turkish papers published at Constantinople are read as far East as Kashgar.

Jahangir. He apparently possessed a certain amount of education, and his wide experience of the world had reared a superstructure upon this basis which made him an interesting companion for Jahangir's soberer moments. In addition, Hawkins was an Elizabethan sailor, by no means likely, as Mr Lane-Poole puts it, "to be shocked at an extra allowance of grog."* This was of the utmost importance, as whatever Jahangir was in the daytime, in the evening he was nothing more or less than a jovial and tipsy swiller of the most pronounced type. Hawkins was equally at home with him, whether he was discussing some grave matter of state, or drowning his cares in the cup of oblivion. The consequence was that for two years Hawkins was in continuous favour, and frequent companionship, with the "Great Mogul." Jahangir made him marry a young Armenian lady who was in Agra, that she might cook his meals and so avert all fear of poison. Mukarrab Khan was summoned from Surat and compelled to disgorge the booty which he had seized from Hawkins on his first arrival. Mukarrab Khan and the Portuguese at last joined forces, and, by dint of a vast amount of misrepresentation, convinced the king that if he granted the English permission to trade at Surat, the hostility of the Portuguese would cause his ports to lose all their commerce; since

* Lane-Poole's *Medieval India*, p. 301.

the Portuguese would neither trade themselves nor allow others to trade if their wishes were disregarded. In spite of Hawkins's utmost efforts he could not persuade the monarch to rescind a decree that " the English should come no more"; and though Jahangir pressed the sailor to remain with him on the same footing as before, and promised that he should retain all his emoluments and privileges, Hawkins refused to separate his own and his country's fortunes, and after a final unsuccessful effort to alter the Mogul's decision, left Agra on November 2, 1611. He was accompanied by his Armenian wife,* and after visiting Bantam with Sir Henry Middleton's fleet, died two years later on the voyage home.

Hawkins was not a scientific or philosophic observer, but his narrative† possesses no mean value and interest. The most important of his pages are those in which he describes the system of life-peers, " men of Livings or Lordships," he terms them, which he found in vogue at the Mogul Court. Their classification was a military one; the highest of the Mogul officers were " men of twelve thousand horse," the lowest

* The original ceremony was found to have been invalid, but Hawkins, to his honour, went through a valid ceremony at the earliest possible moment. The lady, owing to her husband's death, was a rich widow when she reached England, and speedily found a second partner. She took her second husband (Gabriel Towerson) on a visit to Agra in 1617, and stayed there, Towerson returning to England. See *The Hawkins Voyages*, p. XLVI.

† In Purchas. It has been published by the Hakluyt Society, in *The Hawkins' Voyages.*

"men of twenty horse." The system was a Feudal one without any permanent "fee." In Hindustan as in England the land belonged to the Crown; but in England the theory remained theory. In India it was translated into baleful fact. The "Great Mogul" granted land or pensions to his officers out of which they maintained a number of cavalry, and in other ways supported an establishment, proportionate* to the value of their annual receipts. On the officer's death or disgrace the land and all his property escheated to the king, who, however, as Hawkins tells us, generally, though only as a matter of favour, made some allowance to his family. "The Custome of the Mogull Emperor," he says, "is to take possession of the Noblemen's treasures when they Dye, and to bestow on his children what he pleaseth. But commonly he dealeth well with them, possessing them with their father's land, dividing it amongst them; and unto the eldest sonne he hath a very great respect." Hawkins estimated the king's yearly income at fifty crores of rupees, or more than £50,000,000, out of which, it must be remembered, there were immense disbursements, as the Mogul's account of income and expenditure was to some extent the national balance-sheet. As illustrative of the scale of the magnificence of the Mogul Court, we may mention Hawkins's estimate of

* Proportionate, not equivalent. See Appendix I.

the personal servants in attendance on the Emperor, which reached the enormous figure of 36,000. From Hawkins's narrative we gather, on the whole, a rather unfavourable picture of Jahangir. His nightly drunkenness, the family vice of the house of Babar, has already been mentioned. Nor was his day very much more edifying. After prayer in the morning he showed himself to the populace, and received their greetings. Then came two hours' sleep, dinner, and the seclusion of the harem. From noon to three a public levée took place, in which he watched elephant fights and other sports. Prayer and another meal followed, after which he went into "a private roome, where none can come but such as himself nominateth." Then followed the nightly debauch. "In this place he drinketh other five cupfuls, which is the portion that the Physicians allot him. This done he eateth opium, and then he ariseth, and being in the height of his drinks, he layeth him down to sleep, every man departing to his own home. And after he hath slept two hours they awake him, and bring his supper to him, at which time he is not able to feed himselfe; but it is thrust into his mouth by others, and this is about one of the clock; and then he sleepeth the rest of the night." Other unfavourable traits in Jahangir's character to be gathered from Hawkins' narrative are his savage nature and his uncontrollable temper. He took a keen delight in watching the dismemberment of criminals and in bloody gladiatorial shows. Such spectacles were his ordinary afternoon diversion on five days out of the seven. His temper is exemplified by the instances which Hawkins gives us of occasions when Jahangir, in an uncontrollable burst of passion, executed men with his own hand instead of leaving the work to the proper authorities. Punishments under Jahangir, as we see everywhere in Hawkins's story, were essentially Oriental, sudden, arbitrary, and severe. Yet despite all this rigour Jahangir's kingdom was, even thus early in his reign, by no means in the tranquil state in which his father had left it. Rebellious outbreaks were not unknown; outlaws and thieves infested the roads between Agra and Surat; while the more distant provincial governors, whom even Akbar had never thoroughly reined in, practically did as they liked with their provinces, and, as we have seen in the case of Mukarrab Khan at Surat, often ignored the most elementary canons of justice.

Not long after Hawkins's departure from Agra, Captain Best of the "Tenth Voyage" gained a splendid victory against odds over a Portuguese fleet off Swally. The immediate fruits of this victory, which surprised the Mogul as much as it surprised the Portuguese, was the resumption of negotiations between the English and the Court at Agra, and the establishment of a factory at Surat. Paul Canning was sent up to the capital in April, 1613, but soon died, and Thomas Kerridge took his place. Both were, however, slighted, and Edwards, a third, "suffered blowes of the porters," a circumstance which not unnaturally had "bredd a low reputation of our Nation."* In 1615 it was decided to dispatch a prominent and experienced man to represent England as an ambassador at the Court of the "Great Mogul," and the choice fell upon Sir Thomas Roe, an Englishman of good middle-class birth, who had already shown himself an intrepid explorer, a polished courtier, and a tactful and well-informed debater. He sailed early in 1615 and made Swally Road in September.

The Governor of Surat imagined that this was yet another of the "ambassadors" from England who, on the strength of a kind of semi-commission, had made extravagant claims to respect which neither their station nor their conduct warranted. He immediately employed every possible artifice to humble him in the eyes of the populace. Roe, however, met him with an unflinching dignity and self-control which completely disarmed the Oriental cunning of his opponent; and in the end the Governor was glad to promise the ambassador "anything he would demand," and sought by every device

* From a letter of Sir Thomas Roe to Smythe. (In Hak. Soc. Edition of Roe's *Journal and Letters.*)

possible to secure his friendship. The crucial point round which the battle raged was the right of search. Roe claimed absolute exemption, as an ambassador, both for himself and his party; but the Mogul Governor insisted on the contrary view, and even wished to add to the ordeal the humiliation of a minute examination of the ambassador's person. Nothing but the most courageous and unflinching determination enabled Roe to emerge in triumph from the dispute.

This troublesome business settled, Roe went to Ajmir, where the "Great Mogul" was at that time residing. Here he remained for the greater part of three years, engaged in an unceasing diplomatic fight, the object of which was to obtain some sort of permanent agreement with regard to trade which would place the English commerce in East Indian waters upon a sound footing. The journal which he kept of his experiences and observations during these three strenuous years is one of the best known of the Anglo-Indian writings of this class; but it is so limited in its scope that it cannot here demand attention proportionate to its fame. As a record of Mogul court life it may stand by the side of the narratives of Hawkins, Bernier, and Manucci, but the more pertinent observations relative to the state of the country and the people, which we should have preferred, are lacking. Roe, after all, was a courtier and a diplomat, not a philosopher or a sociologist. Indian history, it is true, is a history of kings and courts rather than of democratic movement and progress; but the very fact that " the short and simple annals of the poor " universally remain unwritten as far as Mohammedan historians are concerned makes us wish that Roe, the first really educated Englishman to visit the Mogul kingdom, could have sometimes removed his gaze from the dazzling splendour of princes, so that while giving due regard to this undoubtedly interesting and vital portion of his observations, he might not have left the other no less vital, and, in fact, more human, part so utterly undone. The history of kings is, in general, merely a commentary on the history of peoples. In the East, it is true, the commentary sometimes almost swamps the text; but Roe, throughout the greater part of his journal, regards the commentary as being the text itself.

None the less, Roe's book forms fascinating reading, deficient though it is in this respect. Jehangir was still on the throne in 1616 and treated Roe much as he had treated Hawkins, save that he found Roe much less inclined to join him in an evening revel than the sailor had been. Indeed he sometimes severely tried the envoy's patience, as on one occasion when he made him sneeze with his strong drink, and then fell asleep over his cups, whereupon the lights were at once " popped out," and Roe " groppt" his way out in the dark. Roe gives details of a curious conversation which exhibits the great interest which the "World-Grasper" took in anything that might add to the pleasure of his evening debauch. "He fell to aske me questions, how often I drank a day, and how much, and what? what Beere was? how made? and whether I could make it here?"

Among the interesting figures whom we meet in Roe's pages are Nur-Mahal, the famous wife of Jahangir, who was practically supreme in the Empire at the time of Roe's visit; Asaf Khan, her brother, who was in high favour at court; Khusru, the king's eldest son, whom Roe met once, and whose tragic history is so well known; Parviz, a second son of Jahangir; and Khurram, a third, who even at this date was making it clear that he had marked himself out as the next occupant of his father's throne. Only two years after Roe's departure the sudden death of Khusru, while in his brother's custody, removed one obstacle from Khurram's path; while the subsequent death of Parviz, alleged to have been caused by excessive drinking, at the same time rendered Khurram's succession safe, and evoked against him the voice of suspicion. At the time of their deaths the brothers were each in Khurram's power; and though the double charge of fratricide cannot be substantiated, the most impartial reader cannot but acknowledge the probability of the accuser's case, and in the miserable and inglorious anti-climax which marked Shah Jahan's closing years will prefer to discern the unerring working of an avenging fury rather than the fortuitous stroke of a blind and nescient Destiny.

Out of the vast mass of details relative to court life which are told by Roe, it is impossible to select more than one. This is the curious ceremony which was always associated with the king's birthday. On it he was solemnly weighed against gold and precious stones, as well as against other materials, which were subsequently distributed among the people. On reaching the place where the weighing was to take place, Roe found a crowd of nobles sitting on carpets round a large pair of "scales of massie gold," the borders of which were set with jewels. "Suddenly he entered the scales, sat like a woman on his legges, and there was put in against him many bagges to fit his weight, which were changed six times, and they say was silver, and that I understand his weight to be nine thousand rupias, which are almost one thousand pounds sterling: after with Gold and Jewels, and precious stones, but I saw none, it being in bagges might be Pibles; then against Cloth of Gold, Silk, Stuffes, Linen, Spices, and all sorts of goods, but I must believe, for they were in sardles. Lastly against Meale, Butter, Corne, which is said to be given to the Banian."

Roe was immensely struck with the "Leskar" or Royal Camp, which, he says, is "one of the wonders of my little existence." It was the camp which was erected whenever the monarch was on a journey, and halted for one or more nights. Roe tells us that it was twenty miles in circuit, and that the tents were regularly arranged in streets, with shops and similar conveniences. It may be remarked in passing that Hawkins corroborates this testimony, incredible though it seems, by saying that the "Leskar" was as large as London. In such a tent-city as this Aurangzib spent the last twenty years of his life in his hopeless endeavour to come to grips with the Mahrattas.

Valuable light is shed on the administration of the Mogul Empire by a conversation which Roe states he had with the "Viceroy of Patan." The Viceroy was an officer of the nominal rank of five thousand horse, but he was only expected to maintain an actual standing force of fifteen hundred cavalry, which cost him 300,000 rupees a year. He, however, drew from the treasury of the Emperor at his nominal rate, and thereby made 700,000 rupees profit.* In addition it was understood that he could retain anything he could sweat out of his province over and above the rent of 1,100,000 rupees which he paid the Mogul every year. Mr Lane-Poole aptly points out that apart from this extorted revenue,

* See Appendix I.

which probably reached a high figure, the governor of a province of the Mogul Empire drew a fixed salary of four times the amount which the British Viceroy of to-day enjoys.* This conversation is one of the most valuable portions of Roe's narrative, and we can only wish that he had given us more such items of information. A few more such remarks would have made him the Bernier of Jahangir's reign.

At last, after three years' hard work and vexatious delays, Roe obtained what he desired, or rather the best that he could hope for. "After almost three years' experience of the pride and falsehood of these people, that attended only advantage, and were governed by private interest and appetite, I was forced to relinquish many points." So Roe explains his comparative failure. Inasmuch as he did not effect a treaty between King James and Jahangir, he must be confessed to have missed the main object of his mission. Nevertheless, when Roe left India early in 1619, the position of the English trade was on a far more satisfactory footing than before, that of respect for the English name. Of things tangible he had obtained nothing beyond a firman from the "Great Mogul" to the Governor of Surat. The firman might be cancelled at a moment's notice; while the governor could, and subsequently did, flout it. But it was not in firmans

* *Medieval India under Mohammedan Rule*, p. 315.

or agreements that the work of Roe bore its abundant fruit. He carried no treaty home with him to England; but he left behind him a new aspect of the English character, an aspect which India was destined to know better in the coming years. At the commencement of that fine peroration with which Macaulay ends his essay on Clive, he remarks that before Clive's first visit to India his countrymen were despised as mere pedlars, while the French were revered as a people formed for victory and command. It was but slowly that India learnt that the British were an imperial, as well as a commercial, race. May we not say that the lesson which the military genius of the warrior taught to the distracted India of his day was inculcated more than a hundred years before, on a smaller scale, it is true, but before a more brilliant audience, in the days when the "Great Mogul" was great in actuality as well as in name, by the suave and unflinching demeanour of the Stuart diplomat?

CHAPTER IX

Other English Visitors to the Court of Jahangir

The name and character of the Great Moghul became the common talk. In a few years Englishmen came to see him face to face as no Indian king had been seen by Europeans since the days when Alexander met Porus on the plains of the Jehlam.—*S. Lane-Poole.*

WHEN all the circumstances are considered the number of Englishmen who visited the Court of Jahangir is not a little extraordinary. In addition to the two envoys mentioned in the last chapter, an exhaustive list would have to include a number of factors and Company's agents, some fifty shipwrecked sailors, at least two clergymen, and one professed traveller. Not a few of these men wrote narratives of their experiences and observations, and though not one of them can be placed in the first rank of travellers' records, they all form interesting and instructive reading.

One of the companions of Hawkins during part of his residence in India was William Finch, whose account of his adventures may be read in Purchas's collection.* Finch came out to India in the same ship as Hawkins, and when the

* *Purchas his Pilgrimes*, 1, iv, 420.

latter went up country to Agra, Finch stayed behind at Surat. At the beginning of his narrative Finch makes mention of the many rumours which reached him at Surat of the progress of the military operations which "Malik Ambar,* King of Decan," had commenced against the city of Ahmednagar. Not long after Hawkins's marriage Finch himself went up to Agra. While he was there, he says, great fires broke out in the city, so that "we feared the judgement of Sodome and Gomorrha upon the place." Then came news of the ill-success of the Mogul army in the Deccan, which, despite its size (600,000), continued to lose ground in its contest with Malik Ambar. We hear from Finch that the cowardice of the citizens of a certain town was punished by twelve of them being put in women's clothes, shaved, and beheaded. Finch subsequently visited Fatepur, Delhi, and Lahore, and died at Baghdad on his way home to Europe by the overland route.

Finch's narrative contains a good deal of useful information on the subject of the daily levées which Jahangir used to hold. "Being entered," he says, "you approach the King's Derbar or Seat, before which is also a small

* Malik Ambar Habshi, an Abyssinian slave who rose to great influence in the Deccan after the capture of Ahmednagar by Danial in 1600 A.D. He had frequent conflicts with Jahangir's armies, but eventually retired before Khurram. He attached himself to that prince's interest, and remained loyal till his death in 1626. See *Oriental Biographical Dictionary*, p. 237.

court, enclosed with rails, covered over with rich Semianes to keepe away the Sunne; where, aloft in a gallery, the King sits in his chaire of state accompanied with his children and chief Vizier (who goeth up by a short ladder forth of the court) no other without calling daring to go up to him, save only two Punkaws to gather wind. . . . . Within these rails none under the degree of 400 horse are permitted to enter. On the further side of this Court of Presence are hanged golden bels, that if any be opprest and can get no justice by the king's officer, he is called and the matter discussed before the king. Here every day between three and four o'clock the king comes forth. After his going in from the Derbar in the evening, some two houres after he comes out again, sitting forth in a small more inward court, behind the other, close to his Mahal, into which none but the Grandees, and they also with tickets to be renewed with every moone, are permitted to enter, where he drinks by number and measure, sometimes one and thirtie, and running over." This passage is strongly corroborative of what Roe tells us of Jahangir's daily life. The "golden bels" which Finch mentions are only another illustration of the Oriental facility of personal petition which the Mogul emperors encouraged. Mr Lane-Poole remarks, pertinently enough, that it is not on record that anybody was hardy enough to pull the bell; but we are not entitled to assume from this absence of evidence that it was never used. Finch also throws considerable light on the Emperor's savage delight in bloody spectacles. "Tuesday is a day of blood, both of fighting beasts and justiced men, the King judging and seeing execution."

In March, 1607, an expedition consisting of a single vessel left England for India. After visiting Aden, and having some passages with the governor there, the captain headed the ship directly for Cambay. Early in September, 1608, it foundered off the Guzerat coast, but the crew to the number of fifty-five persons managed to reach the mouth of the Gandevi, whence they made their way to Surat, where they fell in with William Finch. The governor, not a little embarrassed by this unexpected invasion, first put them into a state of semi-captivity, and finally arranged that they should go up country to the Court of Jahangir, in order, to use the words of one of the party,* "to certify him of our distress."

Of the experiences of this unfortunate crew we possess two detailed accounts, one of them by Captain Robert Coverte, the other by John Jourdain. Jourdain, however, left the main body at Surat, and the narrative which he wrote throws no light on their adventures at Agra.

From Coverte's story† we gather that the

* Coverte. † Harleian, II, 237.

sailors journeyed to Agra by the road which went through Burhanpur. "After staying here awhile, I and John Frenchman went to crave the general's pass. He asked us to serve him in the wars." At that time Burhanpur was a great military centre, and Coverte tells us that it was bigger than London,* and that a flourishing commerce was carried on there. After leaving this place they witnessed a suttee. On their arrival at the capital Hawkins immediately introduced them into the presence of Jahangir, "as is the custom and manner of the country, for no person may stay above twenty-four hours, before he is brought before the king, to know what he is and whence he cometh." The emperor repeated the invitation of his commander-in-chief at Burhanpur that the sailors would enter his service. Apparently a number of them did so, for eventually only five of them set out for Candahar to travel home overland.† Owing to various causes the party, as it reached Dover in April, 1611, consisted only of two men, Robert Coverte and Richard Martin.‡

Meantime John Jourdain was otherwise

* i.e., the London of 1610.

† Their names were Robert Coverte, Joseph Salbancke, John Frenchman, Richard Martin, and Richard Fox.

‡ Coverte's ejaculatory utterance at the close of his narrative deserves quotation:

"Setting my foot on English ground, I thought all my miseries to be at an end. For to me all the nations and kingdoms, that in these my travels I passed by and saw, both by sea and land, seemed nothing comparable to it. But that in respect of them all it may be called the only paradise and blessed country of the world."

occupied. At first he remained for some time at Surat with Finch, and, on the latter going up to Agra, was left behind to dispose of the small stock of goods which remained there unsold. At the end of 1610 he was summoned to the capital by Hawkins, with the result that he spent six months at Agra. His journal, however, passes over the events of this time very scantily, though we can catch some glimpses of the court and the Emperor here and there in his narrative. Declining (fortunately, in all probability, for himself) an invitation from Finch at Lahore to accompany him home overland, Jourdain determined to return to Surat. On applying to Jahangir for his pass the monarch gave it, but assured him " that his passe to travaile was needlesse, because his country was a free country for all men."* At Cambay Jourdain received from the native governor the welcome news that Sir Henry Middleton had arrived with a fleet. Nicholas Bangham was at this time the only Englishman at Surat; and Portuguese hostility made it impossible for the fleet to come into that port to communicate with him. In the end Jourdain with five other Englishmen succeeded in attracting Middleton's attention further up the coast, and was taken on board. To him Jourdain conveyed the invaluable intelligence of a good harbourage at Swally Hole,

* This scarcely seems on all fours with what Coverte says. See above, p. 159.

the discovery of which was of inestimable value to succeeding English ventures, and practically checkmated Portuguese hostility. On the newcomers attempting to trade they met with a flat and peremptory prohibition from Mukarrab Khan; they therefore departed, and after doing some business at Dabul, and harassing the native vessels trading between Cambay and Mocha, divided the fleet into separate expeditions. Jourdain went with a vessel to the islands and Amboina, and after a very successful voyage returned to England. Three years later he conducted a second expedition, and lost his life in a skirmish with the Dutch off Malay.

Neither Coverte nor Jourdain give us any information that is indispensably valuable from the point of view of this work. The interest of their narratives is mainly personal. Coverte and Jourdain were true Englishmen, and are among the brightest figures of all those who pioneered the English trade with India. The eulogy which his editor pronounced over the second may fitly be applied to both. "It is needless," he says, "to pronounce an elaborate oration over his grave. His journal is his monument; and in its candid pages we can easily discern the sterling nature of the man." To resourceful and energetic patriots such as these the British Empire in India owes much.

Passing mention should be made of Nicholas Withington, a member of Captain Best's fleet, who went from Surat to Agra in 1614, and of Richard Steele and John Crowther, who travelled from Ajmir to Ispahan in the following year. The journals of both these expeditions contain some useful information.*

Sir Thomas Roe was intensely jealous of the dignity of his countrymen. He was, therefore, very annoyed when on his arrival at Ajmir in 1616 he received an unexpected call from a countryman and acquaintance of his, who he feared was likely to diminish the prestige which he wished to attach to the English name. This acquaintance was the "Odcombian leg-stretcher," Thomas Coryat, the author of the *Crudities.* After passing on foot through Europe, Coryat travelled on foot through Constantinople, Jerusalem, Troy, Damascus, and Persia until he reached Ajmir. "His notes," Roe tells us, "are already too great for portage, some left at Aleppo, some at Hispan—enough to make any stationer an alderman that shall but serve the Printer with Paper."

Roe's fears were only too well founded. One of this extraordinary man's first actions was to address a Persian oration to the Mogul, who threw him a hundred rupees as a reward. Roe sternly reproved him for this "as tending to the Dishonour of our Nation," but Coryat answered the ambassador, according to his own account, "in that stout and resolute manner

* See *Purchas his Pilgrimes*, I, iv, 519, 482.

. . . . that he was contented to cease nibling at me."

The Rev. Edward Terry was for some time Coryat's tent fellow, and records some of his sayings.* Once he undertook the task of silencing a brawling native laundress, and out-talked her in her own language. On another occasion at the time of evening prayer he answered the muezzin's call by proclaiming aloud in the native tongue that Mohammed was an impostor. It was only his reputed madness that saved him from the fury of the populace. He was extremely vain, and was intensely annoyed when he heard through the medium of a letter sent to Roe from England that King James, on hearing that he was in India had remarked: "Is that fool yet living?" Eventually he started in very feeble health for Surat, with the intention of visiting Africa. At Surat, however, the kindly factors plied him with sack to such an extent that he speedily succumbed to his weakness, and "overtook Death in the month of December, 1617."†

"Sic exit Coryatus," says genial parson Terry, who made a poem on his death. "Hence he went off the stage, and so must all after him, how long soever their parts seem to be: For if one should go to the extreme part of the world, East, another West, another North, and

* Terry's *Voyage to East India*. Edition of 1655, pp. 58–78.
† Terry.

another South, they must all meet at last together in the Field of Bones, wherein our traveller hath now taken up his Lodging, and where I now leave him."

In likewise taking leave of this extraordinary man we may safely say that there is no more striking figure among all the long list of Indian travellers than Thomas Coryat. None was more singlehearted than he in his love of travel. His journey from Aleppo to Ajmir was performed almost entirely on foot, and cost him but three pounds all told, "of which I was cozened of no less than tenne shilling sterling." His remarkable signature, to which no one had a better right than he, was of a piece with the rest of his character. "Your generosities most obliged Countryman," it ran, "ever to be commanded by you, the Hierosolymitan-Syrian-Mesopotamian - Armenian - Median - Parthian - Persian-Indian Legge-Stretcher of Odcombe in Somerset, Thomas Coryat." Some letters of his were published in 1616,* and extracts from them appear in Purchas's collection of travels, but his voluminous notes, to which Roe makes reference, and which would have undoubtedly formed fascinating reading, have unhappily perished. Their disappearance leaves a gap which no other writer has exactly filled. A

* The book was entitled, *Thomas Coriate Traveller for the English Wits: Greeting, From the Court of the Great Mogul, Resident at the Towne of Asmere in Easterne India.*

volume of Indian travel on the lines of the *Crudities* would have been an invaluable addition to early Anglo-Indian literature.

In 1616 Roe's chaplain, the Rev. John Hall, died, and was succeeded by Terry, who has already been mentioned in connection with Coryat. Terry remained with Roe till 1619, and accompanied him home to England. In 1622 he published a small journal of his travels, and in 1655 published an enlarged volume, in which he seems to have embodied, to judge from the work itself, all the religious homilies which he had delivered in the interval to his parishioners in Great Greenford. This he did, as he confesses, in order "that they who fly from a sermon and will not touch sound and wholesome and excellent treatises in divinity may happily (if God so please) be taken before they are aware and overcome by some divine truths." It must be acknowledged that the worthy divine grafts some very excellent moral discourses on the depravity and wickedness which he met in India.

From the motto on the title-page "Qui nescit orare, discat navigare," we can infer some of Terry's alarm on the outward voyage. The journey up country was uneventful. Terry remarks the absence of inns for the convenience of travellers, a fact commented on by many other visitors to the country. He was delighted by the discovery of "a very pleasant and clear liquor, called Toddie, issuing from a Spongie

Tree." His description of his life at Court is interesting, but adds little to what we know from Roe. He has a few very pertinent remarks on Mogul government. The Government, he says, is " that indeed, which is the worst of all governments, called by Aristotle, " Δεσποτεία. " It was " arbitrary, illimited, tyrannical, such as a severe master useth to servants." He comments, too, on the absence of laws. "There are no laws for government kept in that Empire upon record (for aught I could ever learn), to regulate Governours there in the administration of justice, but what are written in the breast of the King and his Substitutes; and therefore they often take liberty to proceed how they please, in punishing the offender rather than the offence, men's persons more than their crimes, aegrotum potius quam morbum."

We learn from Terry, too, that Jahangir sat as judge " in any matter of consequence " that happened near him, a fact we have gathered from other travellers also. Summary justice was the rule. The penalty of murder and theft was death, which was inflicted by hanging, beheading, impaling, dismemberment by wild beasts and similar methods. In the provinces the governors judged in all criminal cases, and exercised the power of life and death. They were assisted in these cases by " Cotwalls," who, Terry adds, resemble our Sheriffs. Contracts, debts, and, in general, all civil obligations were enforced by a Cadi, whose jurisdiction did not extend to criminal cases. Debt was enforced, if necessary, by the imprisonment of the debtor; he might even be sold into slavery, with his wife and children, to defray the debt.*

Terry's narrative makes an admirable complement to Roe's journal, and in its expanded form is excellent and diverting reading, the writer, even in the midst of his perpetual sermonizing, remaining interesting. It is illustrated by apt quotation, classical, biblical, and modern, by means of which the tedium of the sermons is constantly relieved.

> In Europe, Asia, Africk, have I gonne,
> One journey more, and then my travel's done,

said Terry on one occasion, dropping into verse. There is, perhaps, in all our long list of travellers in India, no more pleasing figure than this genial parson, who used his travels as the book of experience whence he might draw lessons that would help his parishioners to start confidently on that journey which they and he alike were bound one day to undertake.

* p. 385.

CHAPTER X

Provincial Travellers in the Reigns of Jahangir and Shah Jahan

There can be little doubt that this great empire, powerful and prosperous as it appears on a superficial view, was yet, even in its best days, far worse governed than the worst governed parts of Europe now are.—*Macaulay, Essay on Clive.*

IN the present chapter it is proposed to deal with those visitors to India who travelled in various parts of the country, chiefly the provinces of the Mogul Empire, during the fifty years that succeeded the death of Akbar, but the interest of whose travels does not, like Roe's or Hawkins's, centre round the Imperial Court.* The narratives of the travellers mentioned in the following pages are therefore useful, in the main, as shedding light on the administration of the provinces and on the condition of the people under Mogul government, and not as giving us pictures of court life and as illustrating the working of the governmental machine at head quarters. The number of such travellers is considerable, and only the more important can be

* Tavernier, who first visited India in Shah Jahan's reign, is reserved for fuller discussion, as his more important journeys took place in the reign of Aurangzib. Pietro della Valle, who travelled during this period, was dealt with in another place, as he travelled largely in parts of India that were but little affected by the Mogul Empire.

dealt with at length. It may be stated at once that only one of these travellers is an authority of the first rank. This is John Albert de Mandeslo,* the only famous German traveller on our list. Two other important names will receive full discussion, those of William Bruton and William Methold. The rest are almost negligible.

Before discussing these three it will be convenient to give the less known travellers the passing mention which is all that they can legitimately claim. Sir Thomas Herbert, the most useful of these, went in 1627 to Persia as secretary to an English embassy which was sent there in that year, and after remaining two years in the East, in the course of which he paid a short visit to Surat and the surrounding district, returned home and wrote a description of his travels. His book† gives a very fair account of the closing years of Jahangir's reign, and of the operations that seated Khurram on the throne as Shah Jahan. Classical quotations, sometimes pointed, sometimes pointless, combine in great numbers with pertinent observations of various kinds to form a by no means dull or unreadable medley. We may dismiss at

* It should be mentioned that Mandeslo actually visited Agra; but as his stay there was so short that he saw nothing of the essential character of the place, while his evidence for the provinces is invaluable, he is more properly included in the present chapter.

† *A Description of the Persian Monarchy now beinge, the Orientall Indyes Isles, and other parts of the Greater Asia and Afrik*, 1634.

once that large collection of journals by ship-captains, factors, and similar folk which exists in the pages of Purchas and elsewhere, which gives us some evidence, it is true, on the subject of the ports visited by them, but only of the most fragmentary character. Examples of these are the journals of Christopher Newport, Nicholas Downton, and, best of all, Peter W. Floris. In Henry Defeynes, on the other hand, " commonly called by the name of the Manor of Montfart," we have a real traveller, whose narrative, however, is so miserably barren that *An Exact and Curious Survey of all the East Indies* was the last title which should have been applied to it. He started from Paris in 1608 and went overland to Ispahan, whence he travelled by Kasbin and Lar to Cambay. In the course of his travels he visited Surat, Calicut, Sumatra, Macao, and Canton, and on his return from China visited " Bisnagat,"* " where the king worships the tooth of a monkey," and the " Realm of Idalcan."† Finally he returned to Europe by the Cape route, and on landing at Lisbon suffered a period of imprisonment. In concluding this list of unimportant names, we may mention a clergyman named Lord, who was in India a little over a decade later, and on his return to England wrote a book describing

* I imagine this to be Vijayanagar, which was, however, at this time only a magnificent ruin, though it was probably to some extent inhabited.

† The " Adil Shah " of Bijapur.

the religions of the " Banians " and the Parsees, which had struck his attention while he was in India.

William Methold was in India during the second and third decade of the seventeenth century. The accounts which he wrote of his observations came into the hands of Samuel Purchas, and were embodied by him in his *Pilgrimage*. Methold's remarks are, within their limited sphere, invaluable. The information which he gives relates chiefly to the kingdom of Golconda, regarding which we have on the whole singularly little evidence from European sources. In addition there are a few remarks on some of the other kingdoms of Southern India. Methold sums up the political situation of the Hindu portion of Southern India in the following sentence: " The first Kingdome upon the Mayne is that ancient one of Bisnagar, rent at this time into several provinces or Governments, held by the Naickes of that country in their own right." In Methold's day Golconda, which by the disappearance of Vijayanagar had been left one of the strongest kingdoms of Southern India, and had not yet succumbed beneath the Mogul yoke, seems to have been one of the most prosperous parts of the country. Its capital was " a citie that for sweetnesse of ayre, convenience of water, and fertility of soyle, is accounted the best situation in India, not to speak of the King's Palace, which for bignesse and sumptuousness . . . . exceedeth all belonging to the Mogull or any other Prince; it being twelve miles in circumference." It is not long, however, before we come to the eternal inevitable contrast, which we meet everywhere in medieval India, between the wealth of the kings and the misery of the people. "His subjects being all his tenants at a rackt rent; for this king as all others in India is the only freeholder of the whole country, which being devided into great governments as our shires, then again into lesser ones as our Hundreds, and those into villages, the government is farmed immediately from the Kings by some eminent man, who to other inferiors farmeth out the lesser ones, and they again to the country people, at such excessive rates, that it is most lamentable to consider what toyle and miserie the wretched soules endure. For if they fall short of any part of their rent, which their estate cannot satisfie, their bodies must; . . . . they are beaten to death, or absenting themselves, their wives, children, father, brother, and all their kindred, are engaged in the debt, and must satisfy or suffer." Apart, however, from this sombre picture of the sorrows of the tillers of the soil Methold's account of Golconda is not unpleasing. He notices the existence of that religious tolerance which was such a feature of Indian Mohammedanism as compared with its fanaticism in other countries. No man's conscience was oppressed " with ceremony or observance." The state of the country with regard to crime was excellent. Murder and violent theft was almost unknown; though, on the other hand, minor breaches of morality like "cozenage or bargaining " were so frequent that " caveat emptor " had perforce to be the guiding star of all purchasers. Though the kingdom itself was independent, we learn that the proximity of the powerful Mogul province of Bengal compelled the King to be constantly on his guard against encroachment or attack. The general impression which we gather from Methold's account is that Golconda was an exceedingly flourishing State, and that miserable though the lot of the ryot was, it was preferable to or at least not worse than that of the ryot in a Mogul province, while the lot of the richer middle class was distinctly better.

Our next traveller takes us to the southernmost part of Bengal. " I being in the country of Coromandell with six Englishmen more, at a place called Massalipatam, a great town of merchandise, Mr John Norris the agent there was resolved to send two merchants into Bengala." In these words William Bruton tells how it came about that in 1632 he made a journey to Cuttack. The leader of the little expedition was a factor named Ralph Cartwright. Off Harssapur, in the course of their voyage, a Portuguese frigate attacked them, and a desperate affray took place, the upshot of which was that the Englishman captured the enemy's vessel. Cartwright, Bruton, and another then went on to Cuttack. Here they were exceedingly well entertained, as the Nabob of the Court of Malcandy had deputed a high official to entertain them. Next day the three were conducted to the Court of Malcandy, and introduced into the nabob's presence. Cartwright "did obeisance to him, and the king very affably bended forward, in manner of a curtsey or respect, and withal leaned his arm on two men's shoulders, and slipped off his sandals from his foot (for he was bare-legged), and presented his foot to our merchant to kiss, which he twice refused to do, but at the last he was fain to do it."* Matters of trade agreements were being discussed, when they were disturbed by the arrival of the Portuguese captain to complain of the capture of his ship and goods. The nabob listened to the arguments of both, and at the finish sought to accommodate both parties by confiscating the property in dispute for his own use. Cartwright was so angry that he at once rose and without a word left the nabob's presence. This conduct immensely impressed that potentate, who was heard making inquiries as to what "England was, the extent of its naval power, and the situation of its settlements." The answers were apparently satis-

* *Harleian Collection of Travels*, vol. II, p. 272.

factory, and in the end he offered the English perfect freedom of trade, and leave to coin money; in addition to which he showed Cartwright great honour in the midst of his assembled nobles.

During their stay at Cuttack the party were lucky enough to see the nabob march away with an army of 30,000 men to join the main body of the Mogul forces in operations against the kingdom of Golconda. We are told the interesting fact that their chief weapons were bows and arrows. Shortly afterwards, Bruton was sent on business to Jaggernat, where he tells us he was entertained by a Brahmin. He describes the religious rites in vogue there, though he does not seem to have seen a typical festival. He tells us that Jaggernat enjoyed freedom from taxation till Akbar's time, a fact which seems to show that that monarch, while he allowed no religious persecution, at the same time allowed no indulgences even to the most sacred shrines or localities. On the whole Bruton's memories of Bengal were pleasant. His final reflection on the people is that they are "notable ingenious men, let it be in what art or science soever, and will imitate any workmanship that shall be brought before them." In the seventeenth century, it seems, as now, the Bengalis had more than their fair share of cleverness.

As a source of information on the political

or social condition of the country, however, neither Methold nor Bruton can compare with Albert de Mandeslo. Murray truly says that he was one of the most active and intelligent travellers who have ever visited India.* The editor of Harris's collection of travels says no less truly that he had "all the qualities requisite in such a guide, Knowledge, Diligence, and Fidelity." That these encomiums are justified a very slight acquaintance with his book is sufficient to show. Being a scholar and a gentleman, and one already equipped with a considerable amount of knowledge about India, he entered on his travels with a stock of information which was calculated to render his observations peculiarly intelligent. In 1636 the Duke of Holstein sent an embassy to Ispahan, and Mandeslo obtained permission to accompany it, with a further permission to go on to India on reaching that town. In January, 1638, he left Ispahan, and accompanied by a retinue of four persons, reached Surat by sea from Bandar Abbas. Apparently Mandeslo had not intended to travel greatly in India, but, finding he had several months to wait before the next English ship left for Europe, he determined to visit the court of the "Great Mogul." He left Surat in September, and passing through "Broitshia" (Broach), reached Ahmedabad. Here Mandeslo was generously entertained by the English

* *Discoveries and Travels in Asia*, II, 172.

factors, whose extraordinarily luxurious manner of life is well described in his pages. Gilded carriages, hung with rich Persian carpets, drawn by white bullocks, and accompanied by horses decked in silver harness, were the least reprehensible features of the gorgeous display. And all this in spite of the fact that twenty years had not yet passed since Roe had achieved his creditable failure at the court of Jahangir.

At Ahmedabad Mandeslo had an interview with the Mohammedan governor, and was by him initiated into the mystery of the secret of Oriental government. Having ordered twenty nautch girls to come and perform before himself and his guests, he was informed that they refused to show themselves unless they were paid higher wages. He immediately sent for them and had them beheaded in his presence. His guests were not unnaturally a little startled by the spectacle; but the governor cheerfully remarked: "Where is the wonder, gentlemen? We must banish contempt by fear. If I acted otherwise, I should not be long master of Ahmedabad." After a short visit to Cambay, where he saw a Rajput widow perform the rite of suttee, Mandeslo went to Agra. Although in the capital, he does not seem to have seen anything of Shah Jahan, and his stay was abridged by an unfortunate and amazing coincidence. While in Ispahan, the German embassy had had a street scuffle with a portion of the populace, in which some lives were lost. When in Agra Mandeslo was one day stopped in the street by a Mohammedan who had taken part in that scuffle, and had since come on to India. He charged the German with the manslaughter of his kinsman, and though, on Mandeslo and his Persian servant utterly denying that they had ever been near the Persian capital, and so setting up the completest of alibis, the Mohammedan suddenly left them, Mandeslo rightly thought it high time for him to turn his footsteps in the direction of some less dangerous neighbourhood. He accordingly joined a Dutch merchant, who was making up a party for a commercial expedition to Lahore, and travelled with him to that city, contriving on the way to shock the feelings of a number of native merchants who accompanied them by shooting some of the many birds and monkeys that crowded the trees. From Lahore, of which Mandeslo gives a good account, he returned by Ahmedabad to Surat, the latter part of the journey being rendered exciting by a number of attacks from Rajput freebooters, who were only beaten off after a series of desperate hand-to-hand encounters, in which Mandeslo manfully performed his share.

Before leaving for Europe, the German went with a friend on a visit to Bijapur, which, ever since it had carved a kingdom out of the ruins of the Bahmani empire, had been the wealthy capital of a powerful state. Constant collisions with the Portuguese had somewhat marred its dignity; and at this time it was tributary to the Mogul power, though the suzerainty which the Mogul emperor exercised over it was nominal and shadowy rather than actual. Here Mandeslo saw the huge cannon which is always associated with the name of Bijapur, which was capable of discharging a ball of 800 lb. weight, and consumed on each occasion over 500 lb. of powder. The story goes that the expense of this gun was so enormous that when the account was presented to the king, he immediately threw his treasurer into the forge in which the gun had been constructed. On returning to Surat Mandeslo embarked in an English vessel, and successfully rounding the Cape, arrived at Gottorp in Holstein in the May of 1640. His narrative was edited by Olearius the ambassador, and was published not long after his return.

Mandeslo's book well exhibits the absolute autocracy of the "Great Mogul" and his officers, containing as it does a number of anecdotes, many of them from hearsay, illustrative of that feature of Mogul government. The succession custom (one cannot call it a law), which regulated the descent of his officers' property, naturally struck his attention, as it did that of all other observers. The "Great Mogul," he says, was "heir general to all the officers in his service." No such thing existed as "inheritance of estates belonging to great persons;" the king became absolute owner. No wonder that in India, more than elsewhere, men worshipped the rising sun. Mandeslo tells, too, a few stories, which he probably had from some one else, which tend to show that Shah Jahan inherited his father's passionate temper and lust for blood. A gladiator, for instance, who had accepted a challenge to fight a tiger with certain stipulated and rather limited weapons, in a moment of extremity saved his life by using his dirk, whereupon Shah Jahan ordered him to have his belly ripped open. On another, who had succeeded in killing the tiger without violating the conditions, he bestowed a title of nobility. Indeed, if there is one fact more than another which European travellers, among them Mandeslo, force upon our notice, it is this, that in medieval India nothing was so cheap as human life, nothing so common as its loss, voluntary or involuntary, by violent means, and nothing so venial in the eyes of the rulers of the country, whether Hindu or Mohammedan, as the utmost extreme of diabolical cruelty.*

* A lengthy and interesting volume might easily be written on the subject of the Oriental attitude towards cruelty. Why is it that in Asia popular insurrection against cruelty is an almost unheard-of event? Why does the Chinese feel no "horror naturalis" when he sees his fellow-villager chopped slowly into little pieces? Why did the Burmese not rise as one man in 1850 to prevent little children being pounded to a jelly in mortars? The Oriental is as brave as the European; we cannot find the answer in any imaginary cowardice on his part. It is said that he lacks imaginative

In Mandeslo's narrative there is an excellent account of the religious and social customs of the people, chiefly of those of Guzerat. Aged people were, he says, always burned upon death; dead infants under three were buried. The rest, it would seem, were sometimes buried and sometimes burned, though there is no doubt that cremation was the general rule. Suttee, owing to Mohammedan discouragement of the practice, was almost unknown in Guzerat. The traveller noted also the existence of "Theers,"* who were devoid of religion and performed all the loathsome but necessary tasks. A dissertation on Mohammedan India in general forms one of the most valuable parts of the book. Both craftsmen and merchants, according to Mandeslo, had a very unhappy time; the craftsman, because the same piece of work passed through a large number of hands on its way to the consumer, with the consequence that the craftsman had to relinquish to middlemen a large proportion of the profits of his industry; the merchants, because of the intolerable op-

sympathy; so, however, did Europe two hundred years ago. The real secret is twofold; it is to be found in the Oriental attitude toward life in general, and toward kingship in particular. The first makes him despise life, and even seek in his creeds the prospect of the loss of separate consciousness; the second makes him unable to conceive of a ruler who is bound by a duty to the ruled. "The Asiatic," says Mr Meredith Townsend, from whom much of this note is borrowed, "no more considers his ruler's cruelty immoral, unless indeed specially directed against himself, than he considers the earthquake or the flood." (*Asia and Europe*, Art., "Cruelty in Europe and Asia," p. 267).

* "Theer" is another form of "Dher." See p. 133, above.

pression of the Mohammedan governors, which resulted in " the only way to keep anything " being " to appear to have nothing." To add to the trials of the unfortunate folk, both artisans and traders, they had constantly to be on their guard against counterfeit money, which was uttered in great quantities all over the kingdom; and the penalty of death was inflicted on any merchant who, to settle his debts with a foreign merchant, exported coin out of the realm.

Such is the account which Mandeslo gives of the condition of the artisans and merchants in the Mogul province of Guzerat. Combined with the evidence of Methold and others as to the condition of the ryots in Golconda and elsewhere, it gives the reader an insight into the incidence of the Mohammedan misgovernment of India, which, though there are breaks in the clouds of misery here and there, makes him feel that Macaulay was too gentle, rather than too violent, in the condemnation which he pronounced upon the Mogul Empire. It is only too true that " the administration was tainted with all the vices of Oriental despotism, and with all the vices inseparable from the domination of race over race."* We shall have occasion to refer again to this subject in connection with the reign of Aurangzib, and in reference to the works of later and more famous travellers; but to realise the abject misery of the ryot and the

* Essay on Lord Clive.

trembling insecurity of the wealthy Hindu merchant, who alike groaned under the heel of a rapacious and time-serving military aristocracy, the student need not, unless he wishes, go beyond these earlier provincial travellers, of whom Albert de Mandeslo is chief. Compared with later writers, it is true, they lack detail, and are less graphic; but the feeblest imagination easily supplies the one, while the fact of misery is itself the rarest eloquence.

CHAPTER XI

Tavernier and Thevenot

Est enim hoc Gallicae consuetudinis, uti et viatores etiam invitos consistere cogant et, quod quisque eorum de quaque re audierit aut cognoverit, quaerant, et mercatores in oppidis vulgus circumsistat, quibusque ex regionibus veniant quasque ibi res cognoverint, pronuntiare cogant.—*Caesar*, *De Bello Gallico.*

WHETHER it be true or not that the French are an especially curious race, it cannot be asserted that they were ill-served in this respect by their representatives in India towards the close of the medieval period of Indian history. In the year 1666 three Frenchmen, whose names are among the most famous in the list of European travellers in India, were in that country simultaneously; a fourth was on his way thither. Bernier, Tavernier, Thevenot, and Chardin are four names of which any country might justly be proud. Of these Bernier is so vitally important that he demands separate attention; while Chardin, though he visited Surat, devoted his energies in the main to Persia, and so claims little more than bare mention in the present work. We are therefore left, for the purposes of the immediate chapter, with the names of Tavernier and Thevenot. Circumstances make it convenient to discuss them together, but it is rather for the contrasts which they present than for any points of similarity between them. Tavernier made six prosperous voyages to the East and finally retired to France wealthy and honoured; Thevenot died on his journey home from India after his first visit to that country, and never saw France again. Tavernier's book is a simple account of his travels, and does not attempt to be more; Thevenot interpolates fragments of historical explanation at all stages of his narrative, and tries to include all India, of which he could obtain information, within the scope of his narrative. In Tavernier's book the interest is concentrated on the author's travels; the greater part of Thevenot's narrative is occupied with historical, topographical, and political information on places which he never saw. And yet the two travellers are not entirely without points of contact. To some extent they covered the same ground, though with regard to the actual extent of his wanderings Thevenot cannot for a moment stand comparison with Tavernier. Slender though the connection is, it yet, combined with the fact that they were contemporaries and members of the same nationality, may be held sufficient justification for discussing the two within the limits of a single chapter.

Jean Baptiste Tavernier made his first commercial visit to the East in 1631, but did not go beyond Persia, which he reached overland via Constantinople. On his return he remained at Paris for some time, starting on his second "Voyage" in 1638. At Marseilles he took ship to Alexandretta, and from Aleppo proceeded by caravan to Ispahan, which he reached in May, 1639. His Indian travels on this expedition are not very clearly detailed, but we know that in the early part of 1641, he was in that country, and visited, among other places, Dacca, Agra, Surat, Burhanpur, Ahmedabad, Goa, and, of course, the diamond mines of Golconda. How he returned to Europe we do not know, but we may presume that it was through Persia. At all events, in 1643 we again find him leaving Paris for India, where he arrived for the second time early in 1645. On this occasion Tavernier made a stay of three years in the country, travelling extensively in every direction. In 1648 we find him at Goa on friendly terms with the Portuguese Viceroy, the Archbishop, and the Inquisitor-General, "the latter having first satisfied himself that he had left his Bible behind him at Vengurla."* Subsequently, Tavernier went to Batavia, where delicate money questions arose which makes him speak bitterly of the Dutch. In 1649 he was back again in Paris, having returned home in a Dutch ship by the Cape route.

After two years Tavernier again started on

* Ball's Translation. Introduction, p. xvi.

his travels. Travelling overland to Bandar Abbas, he embarked at that port for India, but on this occasion went round Cape Comorin and landed at Masulipatam. This was in July, 1652. After a visit to St Thomé, and a business interview with Mir Jumla, Tavernier started for Golconda, from which place he proceeded to Surat From Surat, at the invitation of the well-known Shaista Khan, then Governor of Guzerat, he went on to Ahmedabad. After various wanderings which need not be detailed he sailed in one of a fleet of five Dutch vessels which was despatched from Surat to intercept an English fleet which was then expected from Ormuz. A skirmish ensued in which the Dutch had the advantage, with the result that they continued their voyage uninterruptedly to Bandar Abbas, where Tavernier left them. He reached Paris in 1655. Two years later he set out on his fifth "Voyage." Proceeding first to Italy, where he visited Ferdinand II of Tuscany, he travelled by the usual route to Ispahan, where, owing to the disturbed state of the Mogul Empire, consequent upon Shah Jahan's illness, he remained till 1659. He, however, sent on to Masulipatam the goods which he was conveying for Shaista Khan; the chief sent him in return a passport accompanied by an invitation to Tavernier to visit him. On starting, a little later, to pay the visit, the traveller found Shaista Khan besieging Sholapur, a town to the north of Bijapur. In 1660 Tavernier returned home by the combined sea and land route, and on reaching Paris married for the first time in his life, probably with some idea of settling down to enjoy his hard-earned gains. It was not long before he changed his mind. Towards the end of 1663 he set forth on his sixth and last "Voyage," carrying £30,000 worth of stock, and accompanied by a nephew and four attendants. At Tabriz he left his nephew behind, and, as two of the attendants died, his retinue was somewhat diminished. At Ispahan he called on the Shah again, and having been appointed jeweller in ordinary to that monarch, sold him the bulk of his stock of jewels at the price which he set upon them. In 1665 he was at Surat again, whence he travelled by Burhanpur, Gwalior, and Agra, to Jahanabad, which was now the royal residence. Here, in the autumn of 1665, he had an audience with Aurangzib, making him some valuable presents, and selling him a number of stones. The Mogul ruler pressed the jeweller to stay to see his annual "weighing," and rewarded him for so doing by allowing him to see his magnificent collection of stones—a reward which was the one boon which Tavernier would have asked could he have taken his choice. About this time Tavernier met Bernier, and the two Frenchmen travelled in company past Allahabad, Benares, and Patna, into Bengal. On leaving Bernier, Tavernier went on to Dacca to visit Shaista Khan, who was now governor, or nabob, there. After some unprofitable and unpleasant financial bickerings here, the jeweller returned by way of Patna and Agra to Surat, which he reached in November, 1666. At Surat Tavernier had that meeting with Thevenot which has been referred to above. Early in 1667 he left for Bandar Abbas, and on landing there had an interview with Chardin. Finally the jeweller reached Paris, at the close of the year 1668. As he was now sixty-three years of age and a very wealthy man, he resolved to retire from business and enjoy his fortune. An interview with Louis Quatorze resulted in the conferring of a title of nobility, and this, combined with the judicious purchase of a barony near Berne, caused this prince of commercial travellers to blossom forth into the "Seigneur Baron d'Aubonne."

In 1676 appeared the *Six Voyages*. The book enjoyed immense success, success so great, in fact, that it roused the jealousy of other travellers, as well as of some who were not travellers. That Tavernier's book should have attracted the spite of Voltaire passes for nothing, and is a compliment rather than otherwise to it. Voltaire was a clever man; but Tavernier knew more about India than he. But when we find Thevenot and Bernier ignoring him in their books of travel, Chardin abusing him, and Gemelli Careri, a later traveller, saying that

Tavernier was "a dupe rather than a liar," we begin to suspect professional jealousy. Possibly those philosophical observers were annoyed that a mere jewel hucksterer should invade their province and outshine them, as far as popularity went, in their own special field. The theory, as old as Hesiod, that two of a trade cannot agree, may or may not be true; at all events, true it is that these seventeenth-century travellers are fonder of blaming than of praising their predecessors or contemporaries; and Tavernier has been one of the greatest sufferers from this source. Other travellers' hostility or contempt, however, did not affect the popularity of the *Six Voyages* in Tavernier's lifetime; while it is now generally acknowledged that he was as a rule accurate in the main as to his facts.

Tavernier did not reciprocate the hostility or contempt of his detractors. All travellers whom he met receive scrupulously fair treatment at his hands. The verdict which popular opinion passed upon him in his own day did not differ greatly from that which has been pronounced by a later generation. He lived on to a wealthy and honoured old age, dying at Moscow in 1689.

The only subject on which Tavernier is invaluable and the supreme authority is that of the Indian diamond mines in the seventeenth century. On life at the Mogul court he gives but little information, and, apart from his remarks on jewels, is worth reading chiefly for some useful sidelights (they seldom develop into full views) on the condition of the provinces. He confirms the evidence of previous travellers as to the miserable condition of the ryots under Mohammedan government. "You may see in India," he says, "whole provinces like deserts, from which the peasants have fled on account of the oppression of the governors. Under cover of the fact that they are themselves Mohammedans, they prosecute these poor idolators to the utmost, and if any of the latter become Mohammedan it is in order not to work any more; they become soldiers or Fakirs."* This evidence of Tavernier as to the results of Mohammedan oppression is some of the strongest that we have yet had.

In another place Tavernier mentions an extraordinary custom which the people practised, illustrative of the vigorous nature of their belief in reincarnation. "There are some among them who are foolish enough to bury their treasures in their lifetime, as, for instance, nearly all the rich men of the kingdom of Assam, so that if they enter, after death, the body of any poor and miserable mendicant, they can have recourse to the money which they have buried in order to draw from it at necessity."† A draught of Lethe's stream was evidently not conceived to

* Ball's Translation.

† Ball's Translation, II, 204.

form part of the soul's experience in its transition from one body to another.*

With interesting but isolated pieces of information such as the foregoing the *Six Voyages* abounds. Tavernier narrates them as they occur. He does not seek, like Bernier, to find the historical or social philosophy underlying his facts, or, like Thevenot, to weld those facts into a general account of India. Therein lies the difference between the commercial traveller and his more philosophical contemporaries.

Jean Thevenot† travelled considerably in the Levant and in Persia before going to India, and his account of his travels in that region gained him considerable fame, apart from his book on India itself. In January, 1666, he arrived at Surat, having come from Persia by the usual sea route. At this port he underwent an irksome and "very odd" examination by the customs officers, who, as in Roe's time, were very strict. After paying a visit to Cambay, Ahmedabad, and Burhanpur, he returned to Surat, where he witnessed the interesting ceremony of the marriage of the governor's daughter. At this point in his narrative Thevenot devotes considerable space to a description of all the chief towns of

* Valerius Maximus (bk II, c. vi, p. 10) gives a somewhat similar illustration of the belief of the Gauls, not indeed in re-incarnation, but in the immortality of the soul. "Vetus ille mos Gallorum occurrit, quos memoria proditur, pecunias mutuas, quae his apud inferos redderentur, dare solitos." See Gibbon, *Decline and Fall*, chap. xv, where the sentence is quoted.

† Not Melchisedech Thevenot, the collector of Travels.

north-west India, as well as of the previous history of Guzerat. After a certain stay at Surat, Thevenot started with a French merchant, named M. Bazon, on a journey to Golconda. On their way to Aurungabad the two met the Bishop of Heliopolis, who was on his way to Surat to return to France. After passing Doulatabad they reached Indore, the attitude of which kingdom towards the Mogul empire is clearly outlined. It belongs, says Thevenot, " to a Raja, who owes the Mogul no more than he thinks fit. He is maintained by the Kings of Golconda, and in time of war always sides with the strongest." The remark is interesting as throwing light on the mutual relations of the various rulers of the Deccan, and of their attitude toward the Mogul emperor twenty years before he commenced that long series of campaigns which made him, for a few months at least, master of Southern India. Soon after leaving Indore, Thevenot reached the town of " Indelvai," whose deserted state was significant of the ravages of the Mahratta guerrilla troops, " who made inroads to the very town." Finally he reached " Bagnager,"* his main objective, at this time the capital of Golconda. A very fair account of the town follows. After a flying visit to Masulipatam, where he gained a considerable amount of information relative to the Coromandel Coast, Thevenot returned to " Bagna-

* Now Haiderabad.

ger," and subsequently travelled back to Surat by way of Bidar and Burhanpur. In the autumn of 1667 he embarked at Surat for Persia, and died at Miana in that country before the close of the year.

It will be seen at once that Thevenot's Indian travels were comparatively circumscribed in extent,* while it is patent to the most unobservant reader of his book that the greater part of it is taken either from hearsay or from other books. His description of Northern India, and his analysis of the Mogul empire, cannot be neglected by the historian, and at the time of its appearance was of the utmost value to a generation which had not the advantage of the more valuable subsequent writers. The same applies to what he discovered at Masulipatam about the Coromandel coast. Our authorities, however, are so many that we can afford to disregard all hearsay evidence, and confine our examination of his information to the parts of his narrative which were based on his own observations.

Thevenot's remarks on the administration of Guzerat, and especially of Surat, are very valuable. Surat, Thevenot says, had two governors, one "of the town," and one "of the Castle." Their functions were administrative, but we are

* Mr S. Lane-Poole's statement that Thevenot travelled "over the greater part of India" is, I think, hardly justified by the facts. (*Quarterly Review*, vol. CLXXVI, p. 517).

not told the principle on which the duties were apportioned. Criminal justice was the sphere of the " Cotwall." Thevenot's remarks are a little confused, but reading between the lines it seems clear that the Governor of the Castle was the military official in command of the town, and that he also exercised some few civil functions; that the chief civil judge was the person whom Thevenot describes as the Governor of the Town; and that the " Cotwall " was a criminal judge with rather limited magisterial functions. The first two were the more important and were entirely independent of one another. None of the three could put a man to death without referring the matter first to Aurangzib. Thevenot's account of his experiences at the custom house possesses a value of its own. It is very minute, and is far too long to quote; but it shows that the proceedings which previous travellers had found so trying and disagreeable had abated none of their rigidity.

Travelling in the district round Surat seems to have been rather safer than in Mandeslo's time, though the French traveller abundantly shows that there was still considerable room for improvement. He describes a trick by which men on a journey were lured from the road by women who feigned distress, and were then lassoed by men from a place of concealment.* He

* Apparently an early notice of Thuggism, though the name itself is not employed.

also tells us of a sort of levy which was in force between Broach, Cambay, and Ahmedabad, by paying which travellers could ensure immunity from attack.

In his description of the kingdom of Golconda, with its capital "Bagnager," Thevenot corroborates Methold in many particulars, and also introduces a number of new points. A vast deal of information on the subject of the customs duties, the method of government, and the morality of the people, renders the chapters in which it occurs a storehouse of invaluable fact which makes them indispensable to any writer of a History of Southern India. Golconda's coinage and its criminal law are two of the most interesting points touched upon. As in Methold's time, the contrast between the condition of rich and poor is glaring. The Omrahs of Golconda are depicted as flourishing on the same pernicious land system as that which Methold described, and as adding to their already large incomes by intercepting payments due to the soldiers. The kingdom of Golconda, like all Mohammedan kingdoms in India, contained the seeds of decay within itself and its social institutions.

"Tavernier, Bernier, Thevenot," says Mr S. Lane-Poole, "were all in India in the year 1666. . . . Of the three Thevenot is much the slightest. . . . His 'Travels' are necessarily more or less hurried first impressions, but he had access to some important native authorities, and his statistics are peculiarly valuable."* To compare Tavernier with Thevenot is difficult if not impossible. Thevenot stands to Tavernier much, to compare small things with great, as Thucydides stood to his predecessor Herodotus. To the historian who must regard these travellers' writings as a mine whence facts may be extracted Thevenot is far more valuable than Tavernier. Regarded simply as a writer, however, Tavernier is far more delightful, and just as the Athenian crowd listened with glee to the fascinating tales which Herodotus told them, and left the more scientific writer to its intellectual aristocracy, so the French of the days of Louis Quatorze devoured with avidity the pages of the chatty Tavernier, and left the other to be the drier, if ultimately more nourishing, fare of professed historians. The attitude of the two men toward their work is quite irreconcilable. If we were writing a history of India we should prefer the aid of Thevenot; if we were seeking a combination of pleasant and instructive reading, Tavernier would win the day. To both may be unreservedly applied the remark which his translator made about Thevenot alone: "An honester man never lived in the world."†

* *Quarterly Review*, p. 517 of vol. CLXXVI.

† p. 114 of Lowell's Translation of 1686.

CHAPTER XII

François Bernier

In spite, however, of much constant maladministration, in spite of occasional convulsions which shook the whole frame of society, this great monarchy, on the whole, retained, during some generations, an outward appearance of unity, majesty, and energy. But throughout the long reign of Aurungzebe, the state, notwithstanding all that the vigour and policy of the prince could effect, was hastening to dissolution.—*Macaulay*.

FRANÇOIS BERNIER was a French physician, whose favourite hobby was political and speculative philosophy. In the early part of Aurangzib's reign he spent twelve years at that monarch's court, during which time he indulged his tastes, especially on the political side, to the full. He enjoyed unrivalled opportunities of observation; was acquainted with the leading philosophers of his day; was fully conversant with the newest historical and philosophical methods; and was easily capable of looking beyond the immediate occasion of an event to its ultimate cause. The result was that the *Histoire de la dernière Revolution des Etats du Grand Mogul*, which was published in 1670, and the various letters which he wrote from India to his friends in France, are among the first authorities which the historian of Aurangzib consults.

Elphinstone, it is true, declined to use what he termed " Bernier's delightful narrative " as an authority for Dara's proceedings in his struggle with Aurangzib, except where he was an actual eye-witness of the events he described, but he was obliged to put forward in excuse a reason which, though somewhat cogent, is hardly entirely convincing.*

" The desire of seeing the world, which had induced me to visit Palestine and Egypt, still prompted me to extend my travels."† It is in these words that Bernier begins the narration of his visit to the " Great Mogul," and it is in them that we learn at the very outset that, like Pietro della Valle and many another, he sought in the Indies not spices, nor gold, nor diamonds, but knowledge. It is safe to say that no European traveller in the three centuries under review ever carried back with him a larger store.

Bernier reached India in time to witness the death-grapple between the four sons of Shah Jahan for the throne which had not yet been vacated by him. In 1657 Shah Jahan's sins at last found him out. In that year an illness, induced by a life of continual excess and debauchery, struck him down, and though he subsequently rallied, it was too late. Believing his father to be at the point of death, each of the

* See Elphinstone's *History of India*, p. 596 (note).

† p. 1, Irving Brock's Translation, to which all subsequent footnotes with regard to quotations from Bernier refer.

four sons prepared to clutch at the throne. Dara, the eldest, who was at Delhi, assumed the functions of government; Shuja, who was governor of Bengal, proclaimed himself emperor, and, having struck coins to that effect, started for Agra with a large army; at Ahmedabad Morad Bakhsh likewise put on imperial dignity, struck coins, and assaulted Surat. Aurangzib, alone of the four, hastened slowly. Though the deepest and most far-seeing schemer of them all, for the time he betrayed no sign of ambition. After watching events for a short time, he led his army of the Deccan to the Narbudda, and put himself at the service of Morad Bakhsh, the weakest of the four brothers.

A peculiar defect in the Mogul theory of the constitution made such a lamentable struggle not only possible, but inevitable. No law, and scarcely any convention, existed which regulated the succession to the throne. Civilised though the Mogul empire was, it was yet in general the most vigorous scrambler, the most unscrupulous intriguer, among an Emperor's sons, who ascended his father's throne. Though we can see that it had worked some small degree towards a dim conception of the meaning of primogeniture, and its application to kingship, this partial enlightenment counted for nothing in practice.* Shah Jahan himself

* An anecdote is told of Jahangir, which supplies a curious proof of the

was a third son. Dara, Shuja, Aurangzib, and Morad Bakhsh had long been watching one another, each ready for instant action when news of the king's death should come. At a touch the smouldering embers kindled into flame. The news of Shah Jahan's death, or even mortal illness, was premature; but it was of no avail that the king loudly proclaimed that he still lived. The brothers had shown their hand and there could be no drawing back. "It was, in fact," says Bernier, "too late to recede: not only was the crown to be gained by victory alone, but in case of defeat life was certain to be forfeited. There was now no choice between a kingdom and death."*

"There was now no choice between a kingdom and death." The words are an admirably epigrammatic summary of the situation, and provide an excellent example of Bernier's power of putting a historical fact or principle in a single pithy sentence.† It was not ambition only which urged the brothers to take up arms and

fact that the princes of the House of Timur were quite aware of the lack of all rules of succession to the throne, and anticipated rather than feared a fratricidal struggle between their sons. "Shahriyar was the most beautiful of all the princes. Once when he was troubled with a severe pain in his eyes, he was cured by Mukawab Khan. The emperor heard of his cure, and cynically remarked that no doubt his eyes would remain entirely well until they were put out by his brothers—as indeed came to pass." See E. S. Holden's *The Mogul Emperors of Hindustan*, p. 267.

* Bernier, vol. 1, p. 28.

† Sir William Hunter's paraphrase is likewise pleasing and forcible. "Each one of the four brethren," he says, "knew that the stake for which he played was an empire or a grave." See E. S. Holden's *The Mogul Emperors of Hindustan*, p. 330.

snatch at the throne. Death, as the traveller points out, was the inevitable penalty of failure. But it was also the almost certain penalty of inaction. The Oriental habit of exterminating all possible claimants to the throne was by no means unknown to the House of Timur. The sea of fratricidal blood through which their father had swum to the throne of India naturally coloured all their views of the situation. Shah Jahan, either before or after his accession, had exterminated the family of Jahangir, and so secured his peaceful occupation of the throne; it was not wonderful that fate repaid him by compelling him to watch his four sons grapple in a death struggle for the honour of the right to tear the sceptre from their father's feeble, but yet living, grasp.

Scarcely a man, of all those whom he had raised to affluence and power, dared to uphold the cause of the slighted emperor. It is a universal tendency in frail humanity to desert the losing side; but in the case of a fallen Mogul prince it was nothing less than political and social suicide, not only to stand staunchly by him, but to refrain from joining his victorious rival. If ever expediency can justify blank ingratitude, it did so in the case of those of Shah Jahan's omrahs who gathered round one or other of the four brothers when it became clear that with one of them, rather than with Shah Jahan, the future lay. Bernier, whose account of the sordid struggle is of the utmost value, puts the underlying principle excellently, and enables us clearly to realise the position of the omrahs who were forced by circumstances to choose between ruin and perfidy. "A few there were," he says, "who espoused no party; but with this small exception every omrah declared in favour of Aureng-Zebe. It may, however, diminish our censure of this ungrateful conduct, if we call to mind that the omrahs of Hindustan cannot be proprietors of land, or enjoy an independent revenue, like the nobility of France, or of other Christian states. Their income, as I said before, consists exclusively of pensions which the king grants or takes away, according to his own will and pleasure. When deprived of this pension, they sink at once into utter insignificance, and find it impossible even to borrow the smallest sum."*

The fatal land system, which was responsible for most of the evils which afflicted the empire of the Moguls, has already been mentioned in a previous chapter, but Bernier throws so much additional light on its principle and working that a further reference to it may perhaps not be out of place. The one grand principle, in Bernier's words, was that "the land throughout the whole empire is considered the property of the sovereign." Hence there were no "titles derived from domains and seig-

* Bernier, vol. 1, p. 77. See Appendix I.

nories as in Europe; " there could be no " earldoms, marquisates, or duchies." In other words, there was no great and powerful landed class, which, secure in their estates, cared not if for a time the king frowned upon them. With the Mogul omrah, the smile of the king was life and prosperity; his frown spelt ruin, if not death. " The royal grants consist only of pensions, either in lands or money, which the king gives, augments, retrenches, or takes away at pleasure."* An incident like that of Runnymede in English history would have been quite impossible in the empire of the " Great Moguls." Had King John been a Mogul emperor, his reply to the coercion of the barons would have been the immediate stopping of the barons' pensions, or, if their grants consisted of land, the speedy grant of their holdings to creatures of his own. In John's reign, it is true, as it is true now, the Crown theoretically owned all land; but even in the height of the days of English feudalism the theory was little more than a convenient legal fiction.

Under the Moguls the principle was far more than theoretical, and was malignantly fruitful of political evil. It amply explains how it was that any son of a king was able to find supporters in his attempt on the throne. Rich " Jagirs " were the invariable reward of the victor's friends. The bad land system, too, ex-

* Bernier, vol. 1, p. 5.

plains the tyrannical cruelty of the emperors. Dignified protest to a sovereign was out of the question. If a king made himself objectionable, there was no intermediate course between slavish submission and deposing or assassinating him. To coerce a king as the barons did at Runnymede, and then to continue to treat him as a king would have been unthinkable to a Mogul subject. With them a monarch was autocrat or nothing.* After his illness Shah Jahan was unable to remain an autocrat, he therefore became nothing. All these various evils sprang directly out of the Mogul land system, of which no traveller ever gave a clearer account than Bernier. His enumeration of the brood of ills which it produced cannot be called attractive. His final reflection on the Mogul land question is philosophical and trenchant. "Yes, my lord," he writes, "I must repeat it; take away the right of private property in lands, and you introduce, as a sure and necessary consequence, tyranny, injustice, beggary and barbarism: the ground will cease to be cultivated and become a dreary wilderness; in a word, the road will be opened to the ruin of kings and the destruction of nations. It is the hope by which a man is animated, that he shall retain the fruits of his

* A vital fact, which, properly borne in mind, solves more than one puzzle. See *Asia and Europe*, by Meredith Townsend, third ed., p. 264, and passim.

industry and transmit them to his descendants, that forms the main foundation of every thing excellent and beneficial in this sublunary state; and if we take a review of the different kingdoms in the world, we shall find that they prosper or decline according as this principle is acknowledged or contemned: in a word, it is the prevalence or neglect of this principle which changes and diversifies the face of the earth."*

Bernier has some interesting and informing remarks on the subject of the administration of justice in the Mogul empire, which seek to combat the panegyrics which certain previous travellers had pronounced over some aspects, at least, of law in India. "In France," says Bernier, "the laws are so reasonable that the king is the first to obey them: his domains are held without the violation of any right; his farmers or stewards may be sued at law, and the aggrieved artisan or peasant is sure to find redress against injustice and oppression.† But in eastern coun-

* Bernier, vol. 1, p. 270.

† Harsh laws are doubtless preferable to the absence of all law; nevertheless the following, which refers to the France of a little later than Bernier's day, may serve as a commentary upon his glowing picture of his native land. " Ce paysan, . . . tout de suite, après avoir dit qu' il voyait bien que j'étois un bon jeune honnête homme qui n' étoit pas là pour le vendre, . . . ouvrit une petite trappe a côté de sa cuisine, descendit, et revint un moment après avec un bon pain bis de pur froment, un jambon très appetisant quoique entamé. . . . Quand ce vint à payer, voilà son inquiétude et ses craintes qui le répoussoit avec un trouble extraordinaire. . . . Enfin, il prononça en fremissant ces mots terribles de commis et de rats-de-cave. Il me fit entendre qu'il cachoit son vin à cause des aides, qu'il cachoit son pain à cause de la taille, et qu'il seroit un homme perdu si l'on pouvoit se douter qu'il ne mourut pas de faim."—Rousseau, *Les Confessions.*

tries the weak and injured are without any refuge whatever; and the only law that decides all controversies, is the cane and the caprice of a governor."* Roe had said in Jahangir's time: "Lawes they have none written. The Kings judgment byndes;"† and the condition of affairs had not greatly changed fifty years later; yet Bernier alleges that "they are not altogether destitute of good laws," though the governors disregarded them if it suited their purpose. Bernier admits that despotic government has some advantages peculiar to itself, such as the scarcity of lawyers and of lawsuits, and thoroughly agrees with the Persian proverb which says that "Speedy injustice is preferable to tardy justice;" but his ultimate verdict is that this remedy for lawsuits is worse than the disease it rectifies. He comes to the conclusion that in Asia, if justice is ever administered, it is only among the very poorest, who have no means of bribing the judges and of buying false witnesses.‡

A very fine passage in Bernier's narrative exhibits yet another source of weakness in the Mogul kingdom, namely, the vice and incapacity of its kings. This he puts down, in the main,

* Bernier, vol. I, p. 268.

† *Roe's Journal* (Hak. Soc.), II, 215.

‡ Bernier, I, 270. For an interesting and informing treatment of the whole subject, see Meredith Townsend's *Asia and Europe*, p. 235 (third ed.) His conclusion is practically identical with Bernier's. "If a country," he says, "wants civilisation, or prosperity, or unbroken order, it must put up with Courts." ("The Asiatic Notion of Justice," ad fin.).

to their training and education. Though the gist of the argument is supposed to have been enunciated by Aurangzib himself, we cannot but suppose that the development of the idea, if not the idea itself, is in reality Bernier's own. A convocation of learned men was held by the emperor for the purpose of selecting a preceptor for his third son Akbar, at which we are told Aurangzib delivered a speech which critically analysed the causes of the depravity and imbecility of Asiatic monarchs. Kings, he said, should be as pre-eminent in wisdom and virtue as in power and station. But their deficient and pernicious training made this impossible. Their early life within the walls of the seraglio was corrupting and debilitating; and when they emerged beyond them, they were as beings from another world, staring like simpletons at every object that met their wondering gaze. Deaf to all wise counsels, and rash in every stupid enterprise, they were, on ascending the throne, utterly incapable of performing their exalted duties. They affected to be dignified and grave, though dignity and gravity were no part of their character. Instead of attending to the affairs of their realm, they impaired their understanding with the drinking of spirits and the fondling of concubines. They compelled their subjects to follow them in the pursuit of game, heedless whether they died of hunger or heat or cold or fatigue. Rarely had they any knowledge of the domestic and political condition of their dominions. In general, they put all business affairs into the hands of some vizier, thereby making it to that official's interest that they should continue uninformed. If this minister allowed the reins of government to fall slack, then the king's mother and a set of narrow-minded and degraded eunuchs administered the affairs of the country. If Aurangzib really delivered this harangue (and no Mogul emperor had a better right to make such a speech than he), the picture he painted was modelled mainly on his father, with a few additional details from Jahangir. As an unsparing examination of the causes of the weakness and imbecility of some of the Mogul rulers, it is excellent. Another remarkable discourse of Aurangzib's and one which throws much light on his character, is the rebuke which Bernier tells us he administered to his old tutor on the latter presenting himself before him in the hope of a reward. " Show me," said Aurangzib, " a well-educated youth, and I will say that it is doubtful who has the stronger claim upon his gratitude, his father or his tutor. But what was the knowledge I derived under your tuition? " And then the monarch proceeded to blame him for teaching him grammar and Arabic, and " such knowledge as belongs to a doctor of law," instead of giving him a more general education. " Scarcely did I learn from you the names of my ancestors." "Was it not incumbent upon my preceptor to make me acquainted with the distinguishing features of every nation of the earth; its resources and strength; its mode of warfare, its manners, religion, form of government, and wherein its interests principally consist; and by a regular course of historical reading to render me familiar with the origin of states, their progress and decline? Instead," said Aurangzib, "you wasted the precious hours of my youth in the dry, unprofitable, and never-ending task of learning words."*

It would be possible to expand the discussion of Bernier, and of the information which his book conveys, to considerable dimensions, did space allow. He travelled widely in Northern India, and, in addition accompanied Aurangzib on his excursion to Cashmere; and so was eminently qualified by his opportunities of observation, apart from the advantages of education and training which he possessed over the majority of European travellers in India, to form an opinion on the strength and weakness of the Mogul Empire. It is impossible to give, or even refer to, a tithe of his information on this subject; his important evidence, for instance, on the miserable state of the provinces, and on the system, remarkably analogous to that which led

* Bernier, I, 175–179. Educational reformers may find an amusing exercise in reading the piece in the light of modern conditions, substituting "the classical languages" for "Arabic" throughout.

to extortion by Roman provincial governors, by which timariots were appointed, has been entirely passed over. The reading of Bernier's narrative leaves a definite picture of the Mogul Empire in the mind's eye, which perhaps even the short sketch of his narrative which has been given in the present chapter does not wholly fail to reproduce. In the mirror which Bernier holds up to our gaze we see the Mogul Empire steadily impelled towards its doom by a multitude of various evils. Its emperors were weak, vacillating, and vicious; its chief men opportunists and time-servers; its provincial governors rapacious, oppressive, and ambitious; its military leaders corrupt, luxurious, and destitute of energy; its rank and file demoralised and spiritless; its peasantry crushed beneath more than Verrine extortion; its judges arbitrary and uncontrolled, save possibly by the king himself in capital cases. And yet, it is clear from Bernier, all these evils sprang from two primary defects, the incapacity of the emperors, and the rottenness of the system of land-tenure, which was the basis of the Mogul theory of government. The one imposed upon the empire all the evils of autocracy with none of its corresponding advantages; the other made the life-peers the slaves of the king's pleasure, and crushed out all individuality, and the peasants the slaves of the timariots, and kept them always on the verge of starvation. The reign of Akbar showed that, given a strong and prudent king, the second cause of weakness, though ultimately bad in its effects, was not irretrievably pernicious; the reigns of his two successors showed that, given only a moderately strong monarch, decay was bound to proceed steadily; while the reign of Aurangzib, especially when considered in the light of both previous and subsequent history, showed that after decay had reached a certain stage even the strongest and most vigorous personality could not arrest its rapid course. The deterioration in the breed of its kings was doubtless due, in the main, to the softness which India begets; for it is a significant fact that India was never ruled well till it was ruled from without. Given time India always corrupts.* But it was not only the enervating Indian sun and the slothful fertility of its fat plains that changed the vigorous independent hillmen of Babar into the delicate and cringing crowd which marched against Sivaji accompanied by a vast assembly of palanquins and women.† India corrupted its thousands; the Mogul theory of government its ten thousands. The sturdy good sense bred by a colder climate saved the west from the practical

* The admixture of Turki and Hindu blood, due to the practice adopted by the Mogul Emperors of marrying Hindu wives, was doubtless an important contributory cause of the growing degeneracy of the House of Timur in India.

† "The ancestors of Aurungzeb," says Sir William Hunter, "were ruddy men in boots. The courtiers among whom Aurungzeb grew up were pale persons in petticoats." See *The Mogul Emperors of Hindustan*, by E. S. Holden, p. 319.

application of the Mogul system of landholding, though it possessed its theory; the East accepted it without reservation, together with all its fatal consequences. It is owing to Bernier, more than to any other traveller of his time, that the critic is able to put his finger unerringly on the two deadly sources of weakness which broke up the empire of the Moguls, and eventually rendered possible an empire larger than any Mogul had ever dared to believe within the bounds of conceivable practicability. "The Great Mogul," says Bernier, in one of his admirably pregnant phrases, "is a foreigner in Hindustan." So, too, are the present rulers of India. India seems destined still for many years to come to rely for her administration, in part, at least, upon a foreign state. Whatever the vicissitudes, however, may be through which India has yet to pass—and the prospect is sometimes a little terrifying—she may at least, with some well-grounded confidence that her petition will be granted, utter a prayer that her misery may never exceed that which Bernier saw and described so well.

CHAPTER XIII

Niccolao Manucci

> I cannot rest from travel: I will drink
> Life to the lees: all times I have enjoyed
> Greatly, have suffered greatly . . . .
> . . . I am become a name;
> For always roaming with a hungry heart
> Much have I seen and known; cities of men
> And manners, climates, councils, governments.
>
> —*Tennyson*, "*Ulysses.*"

IT is doubtful which of the two travellers, Thomas Coryat and Niccolao Manucci, is entitled to the distinction of being the most extraordinary figure in all the long list of European travellers who visited India between the irruption of Timur and the death of Aurangzib. Perhaps on the whole Coryat bears off the palm, but Manucci is not far behind him. In all other respects, of course, there is no comparison between the two men. Coryat spent only a few months in India, and left no record of his observations; Manucci spent a lifetime there, and wrote a book of the highest value.

The history of this book, or rather manuscript, which never saw print till the year 1907, is one of the many literary romances which have been the lot of our travellers' records. Catrou, the French historian of the Mogul Empire, who wrote in 1705, had access to Manucci's original manuscript, and, though he drew from other sources as well, made Manucci's record the "fondement" of his work. Manucci's manuscript then disappeared; and subsequent writers, in quoting Catrou, notably Robert Orme and Mr S. Lane-Poole, have lamented the fact that they had no means of authenticating Catrou's history by a reference to the source from which he derived most of his facts. Mr Lane-Poole, writing in 1893, and judging by the impression which he had formed of Manucci's work from the version of it in Catrou's history, said that he considered the vanished manuscript to be a work full of errors, to savour strongly of the "chronique scandaleuse," and to be the production of a disappointed underling. He added, however, that the discovery of Manucci's narrative would make Catrou's history invaluable, as it would then be possible to authenticate it by collating it with his sources.* A few years ago the *Storia do Mogor* at last came to light at Berlin, having been forgotten rather than lost during the long interval; and the excellent edition published in the Indian Text Series has rendered reference to Catrou a work of supererogation. Written originally partly in Italian, partly in French, and partly in Portuguese, it has now been translated

* Mr Lane-Poole's *Aurangzib*, in the Preface.

into English,* and practically renders all histories of Aurangzib's reign to some extent deficient.

Niccolao Manucci was a native of Venice. In 1653, at the age of fourteen, he ran away from home, and, having entered the service of a certain Viscount Bellemont, accompanied him via Smyrna and Ispahan to Gombron, whence the two sailed to Surat, reaching that port in January, 1656. Not long after, they left by the usual route through Burhanpur and Gwalior for Agra, which they reached safely; but in the course of their journey to Delhi, where the Mogul Court had now taken up its residence, Bellemont died. Manucci, who was still little more than a boy, was now masterless. The struggle, however, between Dara on the one side and Aurangzib and Morad Bakhsh on the other, had just begun, and Manucci had no difficulty in obtaining a position as artilleryman in Dara's army. As Bernier was at this time in the retinue of Aurangzib, it happens that we are in possession of two independent European accounts of the battle of Samugarh, written from opposite points of view. The result of the engagement destroyed all Dara's hopes of a throne, and Manucci, who apparently cut no very heroic figure in the conflict, fled to Agra, and attached himself in disguise to the army of the victorious Aurangzib. After witnessing Aurangzib's seizure of Morad Bakhsh, he re-at-

*By William Irvine, late Bengal Civil Service.

tached himself to Dara, who was now at Lahore, and accompanied him to Multan and Bhakhar. He was now appointed captain of Dara's artillery, but upon the capture and execution of Dara was again thrown out of employment; and, as his dislike of Aurangzib prevented him joining that prince, he remained so for some short time. After again visiting Delhi and Agra, and travelling in Bengal, Manucci, in the true spirit of the Jack-of-all-trades which he was, blossomed forth into a quack doctor. Finding medicine distasteful, or not sufficiently lucrative or exciting, he again took up the profession of arms, this time in the service of Rajah Jai Singh;* and, in his capacity of captain of artillery, accompanied Jai Singh into the Deccan, on that leader's appointment to a governorship there. At Aurungabad, where Jai Singh amalgamated his forces with those of Shah Alam, Manucci saw, for the first time, the famous Mahratta chief, Sivaji. This was in June, 1665. After some operations against Bijapur, Manucci resigned his commission, and made his way to Bassain, north of Bombay, where he narrowly escaped the clutches of the inquisition, which was then in full operation in Portuguese India. After a fifteen months' stay at Goa, he left the town, disguised as a

* Jai Singh I (Rajah). Served under Shah Jahan; and was made governor of the conquered provinces of the Deccan about 1664 A.D. by Aurangzib. Recalled to court in 1666, but died at Burhanpur. Was one of the most cultured of the Rajputs, understanding, besides Hindi, the three languages, Turki, Persian, and Arabic. See *Oriental Biog. Dict.* p. 193.

Portuguese Carmelite friar, and made his way to Agra and Delhi. Manucci now spent six or seven years at Lahore, and gained a small fortune by his fees for medical advice. He now determined to settle down and enjoy his competency, and selected Salsette island as the place of his retreat. An unfortunate commercial speculation swallowing up all he possessed, Manucci, after a short period of quiescence, was compelled to become a wanderer again. Returning to Delhi, he was lucky enough to cure a wife of Shah Alam of an affliction of the ear, and was immediately appointed one of that official's physicians. In 1678 Shah Alam was made governor of the Deccan, and Manucci accompanied him there in his professional capacity; but soon returned with him to Northern India, as Aurangzib recalled the new governor almost at once in order to help him in the conquest of Jodhpur. In 1681 Aurangzib left his capital, which he was destined never to see again. Realising that if the South was ever to be rescued from the Mahratta plague, he must lead his armies in person against the infidels, he mustered an immense host, and set out upon that extraordinary series of campaigns in the Deccan and Southern India which ended only with his death in 1707. Already grey-haired and grey-bearded when he started, the lonely old man had yet twenty-six years of strenuous yet fruitless toil before him.

Niccolao Manucci

Before Aurangzib's first campaign, Manucci abandoned the service of Shah Alam, and, reaching Surat, made his way by boat to Daman and Goa. The Portuguese Viceroy had but recently been defeated by Sambaji, Sivaji's successor, in a skirmish, and eagerly availed himself of Manucci's services with a view to the negotiation of an agreement, though all the Venetian's endeavours came to nothing. Further losses befalling the Portuguese, Manucci was again despatched on an embassy, to Shah Alam as well as to the Mahratta chief. For his excellent manipulation of these embassies Manucci was, in 1684, created a knight of the Portuguese Order of St Jago. On a second ambassadorial visit to Shah Alam, however, the new knight was detained by that nabob as a deserter from his service; but Manucci, after a first abortive attempt at flight, succeeded eventually in escaping to Golconda. Shah Alam subsequently occupied Golconda, and Manucci was for a time in a condition of the utmost peril; but, after various adventures, in the course of which he was once actually captured by the Shah's soldiers, he found a safe refuge at Madras, which he reached in 1686. The versatile knight now found yet another occupation, entering the service of the English governor, Gyfford, as foreign correspondent, and being employed chiefly in managing the governor's correspondence with Aurangzib. Governors Yale and Higginson (1687–1698), who succeeded Gyfford, were less well inclined towards the adventurer, but on Thomas Pitt's appointment to the post of governor in 1698 Manucci's prospects once more improved. On the foundation of a rival English company in 1700 Manucci was offered, and declined, a lucrative post as interpreter which it offered him. Subsequently the Governor and Council of Madras recognised his services by making him a grant of leasehold land in perpetuity in the city, together with a house which was standing upon it. He died in 1717, at the age of eighty-four.

Such a chequered and adventurous career must be almost unique in the annals of Indian travel, home of romance though that country was in the seventeenth century. Probably few Europeans, if any, who have ever found a career in India, have played so many parts as he. The extraordinary length of his career adds to its interest. Manucci fought in the battle that made Aurangzib master of the Mogul Empire, and, in spite of that monarch's long reign of fifty years, outlived four of his successors. But there was one rôle more which this man of many rôles desired to play. Not content with having been captain of artillery to a Mogul prince, physician in ordinary to a provincial governor, plenipotentiary of a Portuguese viceroy, retired country gentleman at Salsette, and foreign correspondent to a British Governor at Madras, he aspired to become a man of letters. The fruit of this aspiration was his *Storia do Mogor*, which, combined with the romance of his life, makes him the most interesting, if not the most remarkable, figure of all the interesting and remarkable figures who appear in these pages.

This work is one of the most extraordinary documents bearing on Indian history that we possess. To begin with, it is, as already intimated, written in three languages, Italian, Portuguese, and French, a circumstance due to the author's difficulties with amanuenses. As a history, it is, as Mr Irvine, its editor, says, " a somewhat mingled yarn," comprising, among other items of information, a vivacious account of the author's travels, which is scattered here and there in the history proper, a chronicle of previous Mogul kings, a valuable treatise on the Mogul court, administration, and institutions, absurd supposed extracts from official chronicles, a useful description of the rest of India outside the Mogul dominions, and a full and important account of all Aurangzib's and part of Shah Jahan's reign. Nothing could be more unjust than Governor Pitt's colloquial description of the work as a " history of Tom Thumb."* For the closing years of Shah Jahan and for all Aurangzib's reign Manucci is, as Mr Irvine remarks, " a writer who cannot be ignored." It is true, as both Mr Irvine and Mr Lane-Poole

* Governor Pitt to Mr Woolley, Sec. at the India House, Oct. 19, 1701. See Yule's *Diary of Sir W. Hedges*, II, cclxviii, note 3.

admit, that much of the history savours of backstairs gossip. But it is for that very reason all the more valuable. "Oriental history," says Mr Irvine, "as tricked out by venal or fulsome pens, tell us little or nothing of the real character of the actors in it, or of the inner courses of events, and a writer like Manucci supplies us with the necessary correction of lifelike, if at times sordid, detail."*

No amount of quotation can adequately convey an idea of the value of the book to the historian. Owing to the already excellent knowledge which we possess in the pages of Bernier and others, not to mention the Mohammedan writers, most of what Manucci tells us is necessarily only an amplification of what we knew before. We already knew, for instance, that Aurangzib was essentially a Puritan emperor. Manucci enables us to realise what Aurangzib's rule meant to his gayer subjects, when he tells us of his edicts against certain pleasures and indulgences, such as those against bhang, excessive music, and long beards. What a contrast Aurangzib was in this respect to his people may be gathered from a delightfully characteristic passage of Manucci's narrative. "It was so common," he says, "to drink spirits when Aurangzib ascended the throne, that one day he said in a passion that in all Hindustan no more than two men could be found who did

* Introduction to *Storia do Mogor.*

not drink, namely himself and 'Abd-ul-wahlāb, the chief quāzi appointed by him. . . . But with respect to 'Abd-ul-wahlāb he was in error, for I myself sent him every day a bottle of spirits, which he drank in secret so that the king did not find it out."*

Bernier and others enable us to see the unhappy condition of the ryots under Mohammedan rule. That they fared no better under their own Hindu rajahs is abundantly clear from Manucci's narrative. Referring to the conditions of land-tenure under the Hindu princes, he says: "All land belongs to the crown; no individual has, as his own, field or estate, or any property whatever, that he can bequeath to his children. . . . At the beginning of the year, which is in June, the officers come from the court to the villages, and compel the peasants to take up land at a certain rate. This bargain made, they must give notice at harvest time to the king's officers, for without their permission they may not harvest the grain. As soon as notice is received the officers proceed to the spot, and, before allowing the crop to be cut, they ask the cultivators whether they are willing to give a half or a third more than they have contracted for at the beginning of the year. Should the cultivators agree to this, writings are drawn up and security taken; but, after having made the bargain, they usually find that what they gather in

* Vol. II, p. 5.

does not suffice to meet the king's rent. It thus happens more often than not that they find themselves ruined by this revenue payment."* This pitiful picture is followed by a graphic account of the horrible practices of people who farmed out the revenue, and of the tortures suffered by the ryots. We do not wonder at the fact, mentioned above as having been told us by Tavernier, that sometimes whole districts were deserted, the wretched peasants finding it preferable to starve in the woods rather than till the land on these impossible conditions.

Space forbids any further quotations from Manucci's narrative. The two passages already given may perhaps serve to convey some idea of his style, and of the kind of information which he gives in his book. A detailed analysis of his work is impossible here, as it would resolve itself into a history of Aurangzib's reign; in addition to which his history rather amplifies our previous knowledge than gives us new.

Manucci was not, of course, a cultivated observer like Bernier, and he naturally prefers to record his observations than to draw generalised conclusions from them. For the task he set himself his shrewd mother wit eminently fitted him. The native talent of the man may be gathered from his medical success. It is true, of course, that among the blind the one-eyed man is king; but that Manucci, without any

* Vol. III, 46.

training whatever, should have been able to become a tolerable practitioner is no small testimony to his cleverness. But apart from the mass of facts which the Venetian presents to us, his work possesses distinct value as literature. From beginning to end it is alive with the writer's personality, and is constantly lit up by a flash of his wit. " No fair-minded reader," says Mr Irvine, truly enough, " ought to say that Manucci is, for many pages together, so dull as to be uninteresting or unreadable." It is this combination of subjective interest and objective fact that makes Manucci so peculiarly attractive a writer. Bernier's observations are priceless, but the cold philosophical standpoint of the author robs his book of the warmth which pervades the writings of many less able travellers than he. Tavernier's *Six Voyages* is often so personal as to lose all objective value. Manucci's *Storia do Mogor* is both pregnant with fact and aglow with the author's personality. It is not for that reason necessarily more valuable to the historian than the accounts of Manucci's famous French contemporaries; but the combination of a certain amount of the virtues of both those writers renders it more interesting to the average reader. Bernier appeals to the philosophic historian; Tavernier to the armchair reader who regards a book as a pleasant method of passing the time; Manucci to the man who reads with the combined object of instruction and diversion. The question which is the most valuable is a matter of the interpretation of the word, and may be left to dialecticians to decide. Each in his own sphere is unrivalled. From the point of view which the present work pre-supposes, Bernier and Manucci must contest the palm. If they are judged by their skill in arranging their facts and in synthetising them into a complete and well-balanced picture, Manucci is not worthy to be mentioned in the same breath with Bernier; but considered merely as a storehouse of observed political and social information, the Venetian's book is perhaps destined to be of more ultimate value to the historian of India

CHAPTER XIV

Dr John Fryer and Dr Gemelli Careri

All Aurangzib's arts and all his industry were insufficient to resist the increasing disorders of the state, which now pressed upon him from every quarter.

A defeat to the Marattas was like a blow given to water, which offers no resistance to the stroke and retains no impression of its effect. . . . But a defeat to the Moguls was attended with loss and humiliation.—*Elphinstone.*

THE history of India during the second half of the seventeenth century was made momentous by the careers of two men of extraordinary force of character. One of these was Aurangzib himself, the other was Sivaji, the Mahratta "mountain rat." Sivaji's exploits, which included the sacking of Surat, came to an end with his death in 1680. But his career had given shape to those national aspirations of the Mahrattas which had before existed only in germ, and marked out the course in which the history of the next eighty years was to flow. The spirit of Sivaji lived on in his Mahratta followers, and, surviving, or rather gaining strength from, the long campaign of Aurangzib, continued to fire the hearts of that warlike race, till, when seemingly on the verge of its greatest triumph, it was rolled back and broken on the plains of Panipat. The scope of our subject forbids us to go further than the beginnings of this great Hindu revival. The rise of the Mahratta power and the ineffectual attempts of Aurangzib to arrest it are brought directly to our notice by the travels of the two doctors whose names appear at the head of this chapter. Dr Fryer's narrative* conveys to us a considerable amount of information relative to Sivaji and the Mahratta power in general; Dr Gemelli Careri paints us a graphic picture of Aurangzib in the midst of his vain endeavours to reach his nimble foe with his unwieldy host. It is not pretended that the evidence of these two doctors goes no farther than this. On the contrary, each of them wrote considerably on other parts of India than the immediate vicinity of Sivaji and Aurangzib; but, as those princes exceeded all their contemporaries in fame, so Fryer's and Careri's evidence for them, and for the condition of those parts of India in which their operations took place, must outweigh all the rest of their observations.

Dr John Fryer was in Persia and India during the nine years ending in 1681. His perigrinations in India seem to have been confined to sea visits to places on the Coromandel and Malabar coasts, and trips a little way inland at various

* A very fair, though short and sketchy, analysis of the value of the narratives of Fryer and many other travellers of this date, so far as they illustrate the history of Aurangzib and Sivaji, may be found in Robert Orme's *Historical Fragments of the Mogul Empire.*

places between Cambay and Goa. For his limited field, however, he is a valuable authority, in addition to which he is an exceedingly interesting writer.

Fryer clearly points out one of the chief causes of the political distractions of the later years of Aurangzib's reign. Akbar had perceived that a powerful Mogul Empire was only possible if it were propped up by Hindu and Mohammedan alike, and had acted on that belief. "This religious bigot of an Emperor, Auren Zeeb," says Fryer, "... is on a project to bring them all over to his faith, and has already begun by two several taxes or polls, very severe ones, ... which has made some Rajahs revolt."* Early in his reign the Puritan Emperor had reimposed the hated "jizya," or poll-tax on unbelievers, the tax which, as Mr Lane Poole says, "Akbar had disdained, and Shah Jahan had not dared to think of."†As Dr Fryer saw, the impost was responsible for most of the Hindu disaffection which harassed the greater part of the reign of Aurangzib, and was one of the main influences which kept alive the feeling of nationality among the Mahrattas.

In 1674, when Fryer was at Bombay, Oxenden and others were sent from that town on an embassy to Sivaji, Fryer did not accompany it, though he gives a very good account of its pro-

* Trübner's edition of Roe's and Fryer's travels, p. 307.
† *Medieval India*, p. 385.

ceedings. Sivaji was found at "Rairee," where he was holding his court, being also busied with "great affairs relating to his coronation* and marriage." Nevertheless, he accorded them an audience, as also did his son Sambaji. The embassy obtained permission from Sivaji to trade anywhere in his dominions, but was unable to persuade him to change the immemorial custom by which wrecks became the property of the coast-dwellers, the real owners losing all rights over them. While the embassy was at Sivaji's court, they saw him go through the ceremony, imitated apparently from the Moguls, of being weighed against gold. On the whole, however, the account of this expedition to the Mahratta court, as it appears in Fryer's book, tells us little or nothing of any value. We gather, from what Fryer tells us, that the fame and fear of him dominated all the surrounding neighbourhood; while his apt parody of the words which Virgil put into the mouth of Dido, in her reviling of Aeneas, seems to be some indication of the feelings which the stories told of the royal bandit inspired in the mind of the traveller himself.†

Fryer has an excellent account of the two cities of Bombay and Surat; but by far the most valuable part of his narrative is his analysis of

* A confirmatory ceremony. See Elphinstone's *History*, p. 629.

† e.g., Part of it runs: "duris genuit te cautibus ingens Jenneah; Duccanaeque admorunt ubera tigres."

the political condition of the Kingdom of Bijapur. This one-time powerful State was, in Fryer's day, in a peculiar position: harassed by Sivaji, and yet glad of his help in arresting Mogul encroachment. He gives a good description of "the disjointed Members of Visiapour, neither trusting one another, nor uniting for the common good of the Kingdom."* In the meantime, he says, "Seva, taking advantage of their irresolution, ranges where he lists." "So miserable," he continues, "is that State where the other Members grow too powerful for the Head, as in this constituted Government of Duccan, where the King's Munificence to the Grandees has instated them in Absolute Authority over their Provinces, that they are Potent enough to engage one another, and countermand the King's Commands, unless suitable to their Humours."† Fryer aptly sums up the position of the Mahratta chief in this distracted state. "Seva Gi," he says, "is reckoned also as a deceased Limb of Duccan, impostumated and swoln too big for the Body; in some respects benefiting, in others discommoding it; beneficial by opposing the Mogul's entry into the Kingdom; but prejudicial in being his own Paymaster, rewarding himself most unconscionably."‡ It is abundantly clear from Fryer's summary that Bijapur was ready and ripe for that destruction which not long after fell upon

* p. 395. † p. 398. ‡ p. 407.

it at the hands of Aurangzib, and left the Mahrattas, after that monarch's death, undisputed masters of Southern India. Without his narrative our knowledge of the nature of Sivaji's power and of its early growth would be considerably diminished. The historian Orme remarked: " Our attention to what Fryer says of him (Sivaji) first led us to discover that Sevagi was the founder of the present nation of the Morattoes " ; and the testimony of later generations to the worth of the surgeon-traveller has been equally glowing.*

Sivaji had been dead fifteen years when Dr John F. Gemelli Careri, the Italian, visited Aurangzib in the midst of his Deccan campaigns. Careri's Indian experiences were only an infinitesimal part of his travels, in the entire course of which he encircled the globe. He started from Naples in June, 1693, and, travelling via Egypt, Constantinople, Trebizond, and Ispahan, returned to Europe by Pekin, the Philippines, and Vera Cruz. His travels in India, which were comparatively circumscribed, occupied the early part of 1695.

On his way from Goa to Galgala, where Aurangzib was encamped, Careri found that travelling in India was a costly process. " At the foot of the Mountain of Balagati, I found the Guards and other custom-house officers so fond of other men's goods that they took twelve

* Robert Orme's *Historical Fragments of the Mogul Empire.*

roupies for two strings of pearls."* It was, in addition, not only costly, but inconvenient and difficult. He could get no beasts for carriage; there were no "Caravanserais at convenient distances," nor provisions; while thieves were always to be apprehended. He slept at night under a tree, or beneath the open sky, and was always, even in the neighbourhood of the Mogul camp, in dread of an attack from the Mahrattas. After giving this recital of his woes, Careri takes care to say that travelling in other parts of India is far better than in this kingdom of Bijapur, "which is constantly harassed with wars." In the event he succeeded in reaching Galgala unharmed.

At the moment of Gemelli Careri's visit to the camp of Aurangzib, the tide of demoralisation, which eventually reduced his army to a laughing-stock, had just begun to flow in full force. To all appearance Aurangzib was a victorious conqueror. The main objective of the earlier campaigns had been the subversion of the kingdoms of Bijapur and Golconda, which paid blackmail to the Mahrattas, and so enabled them to maintain their resistance. In 1686 and 1688, respectively, the cities of Bijapur and Golconda had fallen, and the dynasties which had reigned in those cities had ceased to exist. When Gemelli Careri came in 1695, the Mogul emperor had been for some time encamped with

* From Churchill's Collection, vol. IV, p. 231.

a huge army at Galgala, to the south of the ruins of Bijapur, on the upper reaches of the Kishna. The whole of South India, as far as Tanjore, was nominally his. Sambaji had been captured and executed six years before; a Mahratta army scarcely existed, and the war was carried on only by independent operations under various Mahratta chiefs. To a superficial observer it must have seemed that Aurangzib's long campaigns were coming at last to a victorious close.

Careri's narrative shows the reverse side of the picture. The army, consisting, as the traveller tells us, of 100,000 foot, 60,000 horse, 50,000 camels, and 3,000 elephants, was far too unwieldy to operate in broken, uneven soil against guerrilla warriors. The camp of Galgala was thirty miles in circumference, and enclosed a huge population amounting to a million. The tents of the emperor and his sons occupied a space of not less than three miles round. Luxury and effeminacy were rampant among all alike. Discipline, as well among the European mercenaries as among the Mohammedans, was non-existent. "The Frenchmen," says Careri, "praised the high pay, and said the service was diversion: nobody would fight or keep watch, and only forfeited a day's pay when they failed to do either." Corruption was everywhere doing its deadly work among the higher officials. Omrahs, who received a large sum yearly, on condition that they maintained a certain force, kept only half the proper number of men, and pocketed the profit. The huge army ate up all the provisions for miles round, and if ever its communications with Northern India were intercepted, as was often done by the daring Mahratta skirmishers, it was in the utmost danger of starvation. It is not, under these circumstances, surprising, that Aurangzib was soon afterwards obliged to relax his grasp of Southern India, and despondently to lead back his luxurious and demoralised host to Ahmednagar.

Careri had a most interesting interview with the leader of this remarkable army of occupation. On March 21 he was admitted to the presence of the aged emperor, now verging on his eightieth year. He saw an old, white-bearded man, of low stature, slender, and bowed with age, with a long nose, and a pronouncedly olive skin. He was clothed in plain white muslin, and wore a turban adorned with a large emerald. Surrounded by his omrahs, and supporting himself with a staff, he was receiving petitions, which he read without artificial aid, and personally endorsed. His cheerful and smiling countenance seemed all the time to indicate that he took pleasure in what he was doing. Aurangzib chatted affably with Careri, and took considerable interest in the news which he brought from Europe; and finished by requesting him, as he apparently requested all Europeans with whom he came in contact, to enter his service. As the monarch left the audience room, he was followed by the "Cottwall," who blew a fanfaronade on "a great Trumpet of green Copper"; and, adds Careri, with a touch of humour, "that foolish Trumpet made me laugh, because it made a noise much like that our Swineheards make to call together their Swine at night."

Careri has some very interesting remarks on the Mogul theory of administration and on the land system; a useful analysis of Aurangzib's revenue and wealth, and of the extent of his territory; a critical dissertation on his absolute power; and an examination of the organization of his army. The Italian does not, however, add greatly to our knowledge of these subjects, which were discussed by many travellers previous to Careri. It is as an authority for the condition of Aurangzib's army in the midst of its Deccan campaigns that he is indispensable.

Both Fryer and Careri take high rank among European travellers in India. The evidence of the one nowhere overlaps that of the other, and yet it was impossible not to deal with the two men together. The fact that they were members of the same profession was some, but not by itself sufficient, excuse. But what made their claim to combined discussion irresistible was the remarkable manner in which they each of them fit into the great Deccan drama, which was played in the last half of the seventeenth century before a wondering India. In that drama two great protagonists monopolise attention; and though one of them disappeared from the stage long before the close of the century, yet the glamour of the name of Sivaji cast such a spell upon his followers, that it may not without truth be said that, even after the Mahratta's death, it was with Sivaji that Aurangzib continued to wage his victorious yet hopeless campaigns. The text of that drama has to be pieced together from various sources. Not all the five acts are to be found in the writings of European travellers; but in Fryer's narrative we may not unreasonably look for at least a scene of the second act, and in Gemelli Careri's for the greater part of the fourth.

CHAPTER XV

Miscellaneous Travellers in the Reign of Aurangzib

Well remembering that caution of the poet, " Turpe mihi abire domo vacuumque redire," I have as my greatest adventure thought fit to expose to public view these observations.—*Sir Thomas Herbert.*

"THROUGH the constant relations of commerce, settlement, and conquest, which Europe has maintained with the East Indies, the voyages to that country, and journeys through it, have been exceedingly numerous. It thus becomes necessary to exclude many whom their merit would otherwise entitle to notice, and to make such a selection as may appear most likely to prove edifying to the reader."* In these words Hugh Murray, the author of *Discoveries and Travels in Asia*, excuses himself for omitting in his book all mention of a considerable number of European travellers in India. A similar apology may fittingly be inserted in the closing chapter of the present work, as a glance at the list of books appended will be sufficient to show.† In order, however,

* Murray's *Discoveries and Travels in Asia*, vol. II, p. 159.
† See Appendix II.

slightly to mitigate the gravity of the deficiencies which requirements of space impose, the present chapter, which deals with a number of less important names, is added. The records of these travellers are, in general, eminently interesting, but their value as evidence for the political and social condition of India in their time is slight when compared with that of their better-known contemporaries.*

A considerable mass of miscellaneous evidence with regard to Bengal is available in the records of some of these less important writers. Among those who visited Bengal in the reign of Aurangzib were Wouter Shouten and Nicholas de Graaf (the two Dutch travellers), Thomas Bowrey and Mr (afterwards Sir) William Hedges. Wouter Shouten was a Dutch captain, who, in the course of his commercial voyages, touched at most of the chief ports of the East Indies, both in the islands and on the mainland of India, and, in addition, sailed a considerable distance up the Ganges. He was in the East from 1658 to 1665. Shouten was a faithful observer and an interesting writer. Of him the author of the *Histoire Generale des Voyages*†

* I need make no excuse for omitting all mention of the famous traveller Peter Mundy, who paid his first visit to India (in the East India Company's service) in 1628, and his third and last in 1655. All those who are interested in the story of Indian travel must rejoice that his voluminous MS. is being edited for the Hakluyt Society by Sir R. C. Temple. Publication has already begun, but till the completion of that great work any discussion of Mundy must be difficult and unsatisfactory.

† Tome XI, 264.

wrote: " La Jugement et la bonne foi éclatoient dans les recits et dans les déscriptions de Gautier Shouten. Non seulement les peintures en son livre sont vives, et les détails interessant, mais il y règne un air de candour et de sagesse, qui plaît autant que la varieté de ses aventures." He was not, however, an educated observer, and his information consists, mainly, in isolated pieces of information such as that which he gives us on the subject of the absence of inns in Bengal, and the uncomfortable tents and sheds (" Sarais ") which do duty for them. Of the political condition of Bengal he tells us little or nothing that is worth a second reading. His information on places other than Bengal, such as the Malabar and Coromandel coasts, is of a similar nature, always interesting, but seldom important.

Sir William Hedges and Thomas Bowrey need not delay us long. Hedges was in Bengal, in the East India Company's service as an agent, from 1681 to 1688, and kept a voluminous diary. It is strictly businesslike and, from the present point of view, is valuable chiefly as exhibiting the attitude of a typical local governor or nabob toward foreign traders. Presents, on making a petition to him, were as necessary as at the court of the " Great Mogul." Hedges came into frequent contact with the nabob of Dacca, and found him rather chary of granting facilities for trade. The nabob's attitude was summed up in the remark which Hedges reports him to have made, to the effect that "ye English were a company of base, quarrelling people and foul dealers." It is clear, from what Hedges says, that Shaista Khan was of a grasping and covetous nature. To this other writers—including Tavernier and Streynsham Master, a well-known company's servant of this period—also testify. "He is every day more covetous than other," says the latter, "so that to relate to you the many wayes that are continually invented by his Duan (one of the craftiest men in the Kingdome) and his governors to bring money into his coffers, would be as endless as admirable, both for their witt and cruelty."* Shaista Khan seems to have been an example of the worst type of a Mogul provincial governor.† Thomas Bowrey, who was in one or other of the various countries adjoining

* *Diary of Streynsham Master*, p. 221.

† "Shaista Khān, Amir-ul-Umra. . . . The son of 'Asaf Khān, wazīr. . . . After the death of his father, A.D. 1641, he was appointed wazīr by the Emperor Shah Jahan. . . . Was appointed governor of Berār by Shāh Jahān in A.D. 1638; and in A.D. 1652 to the more important command of Gujrāt. In A.D. 1656 he was employed by 'Alamgīr (Aurangzeb), at that time viceroy of the Deccan, to serve as lieutenant to his eldest son, Sultan Muhammad, in the war of Golkanda. In the contentions of Shāh Jahān's sons for the throne in A.D. 1658, he served under Dārā Shikōh, whom he betrayed by giving intelligence and guides to Aurangzeb. He was appointed in July, A.D. 1659, governor of the Deccan in the room of Muhammad Muazzim, the son of the Emperor 'Alamgīr, who was recalled to the presence, and in A.D. 1666 as governor of Bengal. He kept his court at Dacca, and by his injustice provoked a war with Job Charnock, Governor of the factory of the East India Company at Golāghāt, near Hughli. He died in the reign of 'Alamgīr on May 31, A.D. 1694." —*Oriental Biographical Dictionary*, p. 372.

the Bay of Bengal from 1669 to 1679, is equally explicit as to the extortion and rapacity of the Bengal nabobs. " I remember," he says, " when I lived in the towne of Ballasore . . . a new Nabob was sent from Dacca to Settle in Cuttack, the old one beinge first sent for to avoide contention between them. The New Nabob, in his Journey, tooke all Opportunities to get moneys, in soe much that he lett Slipp none whereby he might Enrich him selfe Either by legal or illegal means. He came neare to Ballasore . . . where he sent for most rich Merchants of Gentues and Banjans commandinge their estates, or considerable portions of them att his owne pleasure. His demands off Some were 10, 20, 30, 40, 50 thousand rupees, and of Some more, accordinge as they were of abilitie. . . . And for noe Other law or reason, but that he told them he wanted a great Summe of moneys to welcome him into the place."* Bowrey is a simple but most quaint† and interesting writer. His chief Indian travels took place on the Coromandel Coast, in Bengal, and in Golconda, on which districts his narrative conveys a good deal of miscellaneous information. Until recently the authorship of his narrative was unknown, in addition to which it existed only in manuscript.

* Hak. Soc. Edition of Thomas Bowrey's *Countries round the Bay of Bengal*, p. 152.

† e.g., Jaggernat appears as " Jno. Gernaet."

By far, however, the most interesting and valuable narrative of travel in Bengal, from the pen of one of these less important writers, is that of Graaf. Graaf was a doctor in the service of the Dutch East India Company, and, in addition to his Bengal expedition, travelled widely in the Archipelago and visited most of the ports of India proper. Previous to his travels in Bengal Graaf had made two voyages from Europe to India; and in 1668, after taking part in the war with England in European waters, started on his third voyage to the East. In 1670 the director of the Dutch factory at Patna fell ill, and Graaf, who was at the time at Hugli, was sent up the Ganges to assist his recovery. As he was known to be a tolerable draughtsman, he was ordered to sketch plans of any cities or castles which he passed on his way. On carrying out his instructions at Monghir, Graaf, who had landed, the better to take his observations, was arrested as a spy, and hurried before the governor. Though threatened with immediate death, and confined in a dark and nauseous dungeon, " fort puante, avec vauriens," as the French translation puts it, Graaf did not give up hope. In the meantime the governor took steps to communicate with the " Great Mogul," a fact interesting as showing that Auıangzib maintained considerable control over the criminal jurisdiction of his governors. A second examination subsequently took place, at which Graaf and his companion were alleged to be "Portuguese, scoundrels sent by Sivaji." Even in Bengal, it seems, the Moguls were not without apprehension of the Mahratta chief.* The two were then taken back to their dungeon, the populace spitting in their faces on the way, but their release was soon afterwards effected by an order from the governor of Patna, at which town Graaf's Dutch friends had been exerting their influence on the prisoners' behalf. After their liberation the two went on to Patna. After a short stay here Graaf returned to Hugli by way of Kasimbazaar.

Graaf's narrative is valuable, chiefly, as showing the relations subsisting between the various officials of the Mogul government in Bengal. The governor of a small frontier town consults the Emperor before daring to execute two foreigners caught in the act of flagrant espionage. On being ordered by the governor of Patna, who was apparently his superior, to give up his captives, he defies him, and only complies on the receipt of a second demand accompanied by a threat to treat him as a rebel in default of obedience. The natural conclusion seems to be that the extraordinary minuteness of the surveillance, which Aurangzib is well known to have exercised over the affairs of his

* "The first mention he makes of Sevagi is where it might be least expected, when he was travelling in Bengal; but what he says of him there has assisted our narrative."—Robert Orme's *Historical Fragments of the Mogul Empire*, Notes, p. xiv.

vast empire, resulted in a tendency among officials to refer even minor matters to the central power, and to disregard the commands of intermediate authorities.

For the Southern coasts of India, and the kingdoms adjoining them, our best authorities at this time are John Nieuhoff, who was in Brazil from 1640 to 1651, and visited India at various times between 1653 and 1670, and Philip Baldaeus, who was a missionary in the Malabar and Coromandel districts about the middle of the century. Both of them were Dutchmen. Their narratives throw considerable light on the growth of Dutch power in Southern India, but otherwise present few points of vital importance.

The narrative of Nieuhoff, who was a servant of the Dutch East India Company, shows that the Malabar Coast was still, as in the fifteenth century, portioned out among various petty kings. To some of these, such as the King of Kalkolang and the King of Porka, Nieuhoff was sent to treat. In these, as in almost all the kingdoms of India, at one time or another, the old Oriental defect showed itself. The King of Kalkolang left all business in the hands of one of his "Residoors," who, says Nieuhoff, "knows how to make his advantage of it."* The administration of justice in these States was extremely severe, and was apparently effective in accom-

* Churchill's Collection, p. 258 of vol. II.

plishing its aim. To the south and west the Naichus of Travancore and the Naichus of Madura contested for supremacy, and seem to have been entirely independent of what remained of the Third Dynasty of the Kings of Vijayanagar, or, rather (at this time), of Chanderghirri. Further up the coast of Coromandel, the sovereigns of Tanjore, Gingi, and various isolated towns, seem, according to Baldaeus, to have been semi-independent, though in constant dread of attack from stronger powers near them, especially from the King of Bijapur. Slaves could, owing to the frequent sackings of cities which took place, be purchased very cheaply all along the western coast. On the Malabar coast, we gather from both writers, the pirates had still to be feared by all navigators. All the Malabars, says Nieuhoff, are "either Merchants or Pirates." The horrible condition of the lower castes in the Malabar towns, which was occasioned by the oppressive and overbearing conduct of the Nairs and other high caste folk, is well and graphically portrayed by him; but, as we have already dealt with the peculiar customs of Malabar in connection with other travellers, and Nieuhoff and Baldaeus are merely confirmatory of them, the evidence of these two Dutchmen, explicit and detailed as it is, need occupy our attention no longer.

A number of other comparatively unimportant names may be briefly touched upon.

Delestre, who was employed from 1671 to 1675 under the " Compagnie Royale," touched in the course of his work at most of the chief ports of the East Indies and, in his narrative, has, among other information, some interesting evidence for Surat, Goa, Calicut, Ceylon, the Coromandel Coast, and Bengal. Havart, the Dutch factor, who was in India from 1671 to 1685, is valuable chiefly for what he says about the Dutch settlements on the south-east coasts; Duquesne, who paid a flying visit to Pondicherry in 1690, is similarly useful as giving evidence of the French settlements there. Carré, who accompanied the French Director-General Carrou to Surat in 1668, returned home with letters to Colbert in 1671; but was again in India in the following year, and, after some travel in the interior, in which he visited, among other places, the town of Bijapur, went back to France and published two small volumes of travel. Though sometimes careless as regards dates, the books throw some light on the movements of Sivaji in the years 1671 and 1672. Carré compared the Mahratta chief to Gustavus Adolphus and Julius Cæsar, so unreasoned was his admiration for him. V. Dellon, a French physician, was in Southern India from 1669 to 1676, and wrote a book which contains intelligence of the customs of the people and of the growth of the power of Sivaji. De la Haye was a French officer who carried out some military operations off the Coromandel Coast in 1672, but the journal which he wrote is of little more than personal interest. In 1689 the Rev. J. Ovington, an English clergyman, paid a flying visit to Surat, on the strength of which he wrote an ambitious book describing India. Ovington took care to obtain his information from reliable sources and, considering the circumstances, the work was remarkably successful; but the excuse for writing it was certainly slender. Not the least amusing part of the book was the Horatian line prefixed to it, which described the author as having seen the " habits and towns of many men "!* Considering that Ovington did not go beyond Bombay and Surat, the claim was certainly somewhat startling. Ovington's book contains some by no means despicable evidence relative to the method and the results of Mogul administration; and yet it is not surprising that in addition to the eulogies which fellow clerics and others lavished on the work, it met also with not a little ridicule.

One of the sharpest pieces of criticism† which fell to the lot of Ovington came from the pen of

* " Qui mores hominum multorum vidit et urbes."

† " I know a reverend gentleman, in Anno 1690, who came to Bombay in India, chaplain of the ship *Benjamin*, . . . the chaplain stayed at Bombay and Surat, employed in his ministerial duties, and in making his ingenious observations and remarks, which he published when he returned to England, for which he received a great deal of applause, and many encomiums from some of his reverend brethren, and a particular compliment from the governor of the Church; yet I know that his greatest travels were in maps."—Pinkerton's *Collection of Voyages and Travels*, vol. VIII, p. 260.

Miscellaneous Travellers

Captain Alexander Hamilton, who travelled in the East Indies from 1688 to 1723, and wrote a long account of his experiences. He combined the functions of trader and traveller and, in the course of his peregrinations, visited "most of the countries and islands of Commerce and Navigation between the Cape of Good Hope and the island of Japon." Hamilton's remarks on India, of which country he seems to have been acquainted with all parts which bordered on the coast, make interesting reading, but are diffuse and rambling, and, in the main, do nothing but repeat what former travellers have told us. His wide experience, however, at times gives his statements a peculiar value, and saves him from many of the pitfalls into which less-travelled writers were led. If Hamilton laughed at Ovington, it was with right. Though the intrinsic value of his observations is not such as to give him rank by the side of men like Varthema, della Valle, or Bernier, yet the prolonged nature of his wanderings in the East gives him a just claim to stand in a category which is famous in another sense, a category in which he is surpassed by Manucci alone among all the numerous names which have been mentioned in the preceding pages.

* * * * *

With the name of Hamilton we close our survey of European travel in India during the three centuries which ended the medieval period of Indian history. It is easy to see that the existence of such a vast mass of evidence bearing on the social and political condition of that country, prior to the changes which the rise of British power induced, raises a host of important questions. What is the actual value of this evidence? With how much caution must it be received? How much allowance must be made for European prejudice or ignorance? What must be our attitude when it clashes with the assertions of later native writers? How far is it affected by the natural desire of the writers to render their narratives interesting to those at home? These, and a score of similar questions, we do not attempt to answer, save in so far as they have been answered in the preceding pages. A detailed and reasoned answer to them belongs to a larger work than the present, a work which has yet to be written. A desideratum among the materials for Indian history is a scientific analysis and classification—something on the lines of the reports on the India Office records which have been published in the past—of the evidence which is available in these numerous travellers' tales. The historian who takes this work in hand will not have an easy or even a wholly pleasant task. The oases of vital fact are sometimes hard to find; deserts and arid spaces abound, over which, however, the traveller dare not hasten lest he unwittingly pass by a patch of green. If, in the absence of a larger and more systematic work, the present modest attempt serves to guide even a few seekers to the fertile spots, the writer will feel that his labour has not been wholly thrown away.

APPENDICES

APPENDIX I

*The Mansabdars**

THE following extract from the *Ain i Akbari* of Abu-l-fazl is interesting as an account of the Mansabdar system from the pen of a native writer. It relates to the time of Akbar:—

" Men, from the wickedness of their passions, stand much more [than animals] in need of a just leader, round whom they may rally; in fact their social existence depends upon their being ruled by a monarch; for the extraordinary wickedness of men, and their inclination to that which is evil, teach their passions and lusts new ways of perversity, and even cause them to look upon committing bloodshed and doing harm as a religious command. To disperse this cloud of ignorance, God chooses one, whom he guides with perfect help and daily increasing favour. That man will quell the strife among men by his experience, intrepidity, and magnanimity.

" But, as the strength of one man is scarcely adequate to such an arduous undertaking, he selects, guided by the light of his knowledge, some excellent men to help him, appointing at the same time servants for them. For this cause did his Majesty establish the ranks of the Mancabdárs, from the 'Dahbáshí' (Commander of Ten) to the 'Dah Hazárí' (Commander of Ten Thousand), limiting, however, all commands above Five Thousand, to his august sons.

" The deep-sighted saw a sign, and enquirers got a hint from above, when they found the value of the letters of God's holy name; they read in it glad tidings for the present illus-

*I am indebted for the substance of this appendix to Blochmann's translation of the *Ain i Akbari*, from whose note on the Mansabdars it is in the main adapted.

trious reign, and considered it a most auspicious omen. The number of Mançabs is sixty-six, the same as the value of the letters in the name of Allah, which is an announcement of eternal bliss.

"In selecting his officers, His Majesty is assisted by his knowledge of the spirit of the age, a knowledge which sheds a peculiar light on the jewel of his wisdom. His Majesty sees through some men at the first glance, and confers upon them high rank. Sometimes he increases the mançab of a servant, but decreases his contingent. He also fixes the number of the beasts of burden. The monthly grants made to the Mancabdars vary according to the condition of their contingents. An officer whose contingent comes up to his mançab, is put into the first class of his rank; if his contingent is one half and upwards of the fixed number, he is put into the second class; the third class contains those contingents which are still less, as is shown in the table below."—*Ain i Akbari*, Blochmann, vol. 1, p. 237.

On page 248 of the same volume, Blochmann gives a table, taken from the *Ain i Akbari*, in order to show the Establishments and Salaries of the Mansabdars. For the purpose of illustrating the above extract, I have selected from it at random, at the same time introducing a few adaptations in the direction of greater simplicity*:

Order of Rank	Commanders of	Horses	Elephants	Monthly Salaries		
				Class 1	Class 2	Class † 3
1st	10,000	680	200	60,000 R.	—	—
4th	5,000	340	100	30,000 R.	29,000 R.	28,000 R.
26th	2,800	188	62	15,800 R.	15,600 R.	15,500 R.
50th	500	30	12	2,500 R.	2,300 R.	2,100 R.
66th	10	4	—	100 R.	82½ R.	75 R.

* e.g., I have omitted the beasts of burden and carts belonging to the establishment.

† Blochmann, it should be mentioned, says (p. 241) that these three "classes" cannot refer to the "classes" mentioned at the end of the extract quoted.

The Mansabdars, then, it seems, under Akbar, fell into sixty-six grades. The three highest grades, reserved for the King's sons, had necessarily but one member of each; lower down in the scale the numbers belonging to each rank naturally grew larger. The total number of Mansabdars was about 1600 (see Blochmann, p. 246).*

There is, however, good reason for thinking that Abu-l-Fazl's classification of the mansabdars into sixty-six grades represents, not so much the working arrangement in force during Akbar's reign, as the original or the ideal plan sketched out by him. Abu-l-Fazl himself, in the list of grandees of the Empire which he gives in the 30th Ain of the Second Book, mentions only thirty-three grades. As we know from other sources that Abu-l-Fazl's list is a complete one,† it seems clear that the ideal number of sixty-six, which corresponded so fittingly with the value of the letters in "God's holy name," must be reduced by half, if we would form a right estimate of the number of grades to be found in the ranks of the mansabdars of Akbar. Under Shah Jahan, too, and later emperors, the working classification seems to have been much the same.

The force under the command of a mansabdar was by no means equal in number to that which gave him his rank. If a mansabdar maintained a force equal to that of his titular command, it is remarked by native writers as an anomaly. It is related of Todar Mall that he maintained a force of four thousand cavalry, "*though he was a commander of* 4,000." Under Shah Jahan, of 115 Commanders of 500, only six maintained their full contingent; some had fifty only.

It is obvious that the system of mansabdars offered great opportunities for fraudulent practices. The contingents were paid from the treasuries, local or imperial, and so it was not so much in connection with these that illegal profit was made, as in connection with the establishments which the mansab-

* Under Shah Jahan they reached the total of 8,000, but their contingents and establishments were less in size.

† See Blochmann, p. 239.

dar had to keep up. Nevertheless, both were made the means of illicit gain. Badaoni gives a good example of the way in which the former was made a source of additional income by the mansabdars. " The whole country," he says, " was held by the Amirs as jágír. . . . The Amirs did what they liked; for they put most of their own servants and mounted attendants into soldiers' clothes, brought them to the musters, and performed everything according to their duties. But when they got their jágírs, they gave leave to their mounted attendants, and when a new emergency arose, they mustered as many ' borrowed ' soldiers as were required, and sent them again away, when they had served their purpose " (Blochmann, p. 242). These musters also enabled the mansabdars to utilise the second source of unauthorised profit, each of them exhibiting in turn the same horses or elephants as part of his own establishment. Akbar was forced to adopt a device with a view to the prevention of such frauds. " The Mançabdars of his Majesty," says Abu-l-Fazl (Bk II, Ain 8), " have their horses every year newly marked, and thus maintain the efficiency of the army, as, by their endeavours, unprincipled people learn to choose the path of honesty." Not without reason is the sarcasm of Badaoni :

" Weigh well these facts, but put no question!"

APPENDIX II

*Select List of Authorities, Books Quoted, etc.**

ABD-ER-RAZZAK. Hak. Soc. Publ. I, 22.†

ADVIS ET LETTRES de la Chine, du Japon, et de l'Etat du roi de Mogor. Paris. 1604.

AIN I AKBARI of Abu-l-fazl. Vol. I. Translated by H. Blochmann, vols. II and III by Col. H. S. Jarrett. Calcutta. 1873, 1891.

ALLGEMEINE HISTORIE der Reisen zu Wasser und Lande. Leipsig. 1747–77.

ASTLEY, THOMAS. New General Collection of Voyages and Travels. 1745–47.

BALBI, GASPARO. Viaggio dell' Indie Orientali (1579–1588). Venice. 1590. Pinkerton,‡ vol. IX; Purchas,§ vol. II.

BALDAEUS, PHILIP. Naauwkeurige Beschryvinge van Malabar en Choromandel. Amsterdam. 1672. Churchill,|| vol. III.

* This list of books has no claim to be regarded as a complete bibliography of the subject of the present work. In it I have merely enumerated and slightly supplemented the list of books consulted by me in its compilation. It is weakest on the subject of the early Dutch voyages to India, a tolerably complete bibliography of which, however, as, indeed, of the travels of voyagers of other nationalities, will be found in G. Boucher de la Richarderie's *Bibliothèque Universelle des Voyages*, Tome v, Paris, 1808.

† First Series, vol. XXII. A complete list of Hakluyt Society Publications, so far as they are pertinent to the present subject, appears below. See "Hakluyt Society Publications."

‡ See below, "Pinkerton, John." I have, in general, omitted reference to the foreign or less known collections of travel (e.g., *Allgemeine Historie*, Laharpe's *Abrégé de l' Histoire Générale des Voyages*, *Collecção de Noticias*), with the exception of the collections of Thevenot and Ramusio.

See below, *Purchas his Pilgrimes*, to which the word Purchas in this list will always refer, as distinct from *Purchas his Pilgrimage*.

See below, Churchill, A. and J.

Travellers in India

Barbosa, Duarte. Hak. Soc. Publ. i, 35. Ramusio,* vol. i.

Baretto, F. Relation du Malabar, traduite de l' italien de Francois Baretto. Paris. 1645.

Beale. Oriental Biographical Dictionary. See below, Keene, H. G.

Beaulieu, Augustin. Expedition to the East Indies. Harris,† vol. i; Thevenot,‡ vol. ii; The World Displayed,§ vol. viii.

Behr, J. van der. Diarium einer neunjaehrigen Ostindianischen Reise von 1641 bis 1650. Jena and Breslau. 1668.

Bernier, François. Travels in the Mogul Empire. Translated by Irving Brock, 1826; by Archibald Constable, 1891. Churchill, vol. viii; Pinkerton, vol. viii. Harleian, vol. ii.||

Biervillas, Inigo de. Voyage à la côte de Malabar, traduit du Portugais. Paris. 1736.

Birdwood, Sir G. Report on the Old Records of the India Office. London. Second Reprint. 1891.

Bontekoë, W. J. Travels. Thevenot, vol. i.

Bowrey, Thomas (T. B.) Hak. Soc. Publ. ii, 12.

Bruton, W. News from the East Indies, or, A Voyage to Bengalla. Churchill, vol. viii; Hakluyt,¶ vol. v.

Buchanan, F. Journey through Mysore, Canara, and Malabar. Pinkerton, vol. viii.

Camoens, Luis de. The Lusiad. English Translations by Burton, Duff, Mickle, etc.

Carré, —. Nouvelle Relation d' un Voyage aux Indes orientales. Paris. 1699.

Castanheda, F. L. de. Historia de descobrimento e conquista da India por los Portogueses. Coimbra. 1552–4. See also Kerr,** vol. ii.

* See below, Ramusio, G. B. † See below, Harris, John.
‡ See below, Thevenot, Melchisedec.
§ See below, *World Displayed, The.*
|| See below, *Harleian Collection of Travels.*
¶ See below, Hakluyt, Richard.
** See below, Kerr, Robert.

Appendices

Castro, Don Juan de, The Life of London. 1664.

Catrou, François. Histoire générale de l'Empire du Mogul, depuis sa fondation, sur les Mémoires portugais de M. Manouchi, Vénitien. Paris. 1705. English Translation, 1826.

Chardin, Sir John. Travels into Persia and the East Indies. 1686. Harris, vol. II; Pinkerton, vol. IX.

Churchill, A. and J. Collection of Voyages and Travels. 8 vols. 1707–47.

Clavijo, Ruy G. de. Hak. Soc. Publ. I, 26.

Collecção de Monumentos ineditos, etc. Lisbon. 1858–93.

Collecção de Noticias, etc. 7 vols. Lisbon. 1812–41.

Conti, Nicolo de'. Hak. Soc. Publ. I, 22. Purchas, vol. III; Ramusio, vol. I.

Correa, Gaspar. Hak. Soc. Publ. I, 42.

Corsali, Andrea. Littera scritta in Cochin, 1515; della Navigatione del Mar Rosso, etc., 1517. Ramusio, vol. I.

Coryat, T. Crudities, 1611 (reprinted 1776, etc.). Traveller for the English Wits, etc. Kerr, vol. IX; Purchas, vols I and II.

Cosmas Indopleustes. Hak. Soc. Publ. I, 98; Thevenot, vol. I.

Coverte, Capt. Robt. True and almost Incredible Report of an Englishman, etc. Harleian, vol. II; Astley,* vol. I; Churchill, vol. VIII; Kerr, vol. VIII.

Dalboquerque, Afonso. Hak. Soc. Publ. I, 53, 55, 62, 69. Astley, vol. I; Kerr, vol. VI; Purchas, vol. I. First publication of the Commentaries: Lisbon. 1557.

Daniel, William. A Journal or Account of, his late expedition from London to Surate. London. 1702.

Danvers, F. C. The Portuguese in India. London. 1894.

De Laët, De Imperio Magni Mogulis. Leyden. 1631.

De La Haye. Journal du Voyage des Grandes Indes. Paris. 1674.

* See above, Astley, Thomas.

DELESTRE. Relation ou Journal d'un Voyage fait aux Indes Orientales. Paris. 1677.
(Delestre is met with under the erroneous forms Dalencé, De l'Estra.)

DELLON, V. Nouvelle Relation d'un Voyage fait aux Indies orientales. Amsterdam, 1699. English Trans. London. 1699. Allg. Hist.*vol x.

DEVITRE. Description du premier voyage fait aux Indes. Paris. 1604.

DUBOIS, ABBÉ J. A. Hindu Manners, Customs, and Ceremonies. Trans. and edited by H. K. Beauchamp. Oxford, 1897. French edition. 1817.

DUQUESNE, Journal du voyage de, aux Indes orientales, par un garde-marine servant sur son escadre. Bruxelles. 1692.

DUTCH EAST INDIA COMPANY, A Collection of Voyages undertaken by the; translated into English, 1730.

ELPHINSTONE, M. The History of India. Prof. Cowell's (ninth) edition. 1905.

EMPOLI, GIOVANNI DE. Viaggio fatto nell' India. Ramusio, vol. I.

FEDERICI, CESARE DE. Viaggio nell' India Orientale. Hakluyt, vol. II; Kerr, vol. VII; Purchas, vol. II; Ramusio, vol. III.

FINCH, WILLIAM. Observations of William Finch. Kerr, vol. VIII; Purchas, vol. I.

FITCH, RALPH. Voyage to Ormus, and so to Goa, etc. Pinkerton, vol. IX; Hakluyt, vol. II; Purchas, vol. II.

FLORIS, P. WILLIAMSON. Journal of, 1610–15. Astley, vol. I; Purchas, vol. I; Thevenot, vol. I.

FOSTER, WM. Letters received by the East India Company from its servants in the East. London. 1897.

FRICKEN, CHRIST. Ostindianische Reisen und Kriegsdienste, von, 1680–1685. Ulm. 1692.

* See above, *Allgemeine Historie.*

Fryer, John, M.D. A New Account of East India and Persia, in Eight Letters. Being Nine Years' Travels. Begun 1672, and Finished 1681. London. 1698. See also Roe, Sir T. (below).

Gama, Vasco da. Astley, vol. I; Ramusio, vol. I. See also Hak. Soc. Publ. I, 42, 99.

Gemelli-Careri, Dr J. F. Voyage round the World. Astley, vol. III; Churchill, vol. IV.

General Collection of Voyages and Discoveries made by the Portuguese and the Spaniards during the Fifteenth and Sixteenth Centuries. 1789.

Godinho de Eredia. Malaca, L'Inde Meridionale, et le Cathay (1613), MS. orig. autographe de, reproduit et traduit par L. Janssen. Bruxelles. 1882.

Gottfried, J. L. De Aanmerkenswaardigste en alomberoemde Zee-en Landreizen, etc. 8 vols. Leyden. 1727.

Graaf, Nicolas de. Voyages aux Indes Orientales, etc. Amsterdam. 1719.

Guzman, P. Luis. Historia de las Missiones que han hecho los Religiosos de la Compañia de Jesus, en la India Oriental, etc. Alcala. 1601.

Hagen, van der. Voyage de. Amsterdam. 1681. Allg. Hist. vol. VIII.

Hakluyt, Richard. The Principall Navigations, Voiages, and Discoveries of the English Nation. 5 vols. 1809.* Also published in 12 vols by the Hak. Society. 1903.

Hakluyt Society Publications.

First Series

19. The Voyage of Sir Henry Middleton to Bantam and the Maluco Islands. Edited by Bolton Corney. 1856.

22. India in the Fifteenth Century. Being a Collection of Narratives of Voyages to India in the century preceding the Portuguese discovery of the Cape of Good Hope; from Latin, Persian, Russian, and Italian Sources. Edited, with an Introduction, by Richard Henry Major. 1858.

* The edition to which references in this list apply.

26. Narrative of the Embassy of Ruy Gonzalez de Clavijo to the Court of Timour, at Samarcand, A.D. 1403–6. Translated by Sir Clements R. Markham. 1860.

31. Mirabilia Descripta. The Wonders of the East. By Friar Jordanus, circa 1330. Translated by Col. Sir Henry Yule. 1863.

32. The Travels of Ludovico di Varthema, in Egypt, Syria, Arabia, Persia, India, and Ethiopia, A.D. 1503 to 1508. Translated by John Winter Jones. Edited by the Rev. George Percy Badger. 1863.

35. A Description of the Coasts of East Africa and Malabar, in the beginning of the Sixteenth Century, by Duarte Barbosa. Translated by Lord Stanley of Alderley. 1865.

42. The Three Voyages of Vasco da Gama, and his Viceroyalty, from the Lendas da India of Gaspar Correa. Translated by Lord Stanley of Alderley. 1869.

53, 55, 62, 69. The Commentaries of the Great Afonso Dalboquerque, Second Viceroy of India. Translated by Walter de Gray Birch. 1875–83.

56. The Voyages of Sir James Lancaster, Knt, to the East Indies. Edited by Sir Clements R. Markham. 1877.

57. The Hawkins' Voyages, During the reigns of Henry VIII, Queen Elizabeth, and James I. Edited by Sir Clements R. Markham. 1877.

70, 71. The Voyage of John Huyghen van Linschoten to the East Indies. From the Old English Translation of 1598. Edited, the first volume, by the late Arthur Coke Burnell; the second volume, by Pieter Anton Tiele, of Utrecht. 1884.

74, 75, 78. The Diary of William Hedges, Esq., afterwards Sir William Hedges, during his Agency in Bengal. Transcribed by R. Barlow, and illustrated by copious extracts from Unpublished Records, etc., by Col. Sir Henry Yule. 1886–88.

76, 77, 80. The Voyage of François Pyrard, of Laval, to the East Indies, the Maldives, the Moluccas, and Brazil. Translated by Albert Gray. 1887.

84, 85. The Travels of Pietro della Valle to India. From the Old English Translation of 1664, by G. Havers. Edited by Edward Grey. 1891.

98. The Topographia Christiana of Cosmas Indopleustes, an Egyptian Monk. Translated from the Greek and edited by John Watson McCrindle. 1897.

99. A Journal of the First Voyage of Vasco da Gama. 1497–1499. By an unknown writer. Translated from the Portuguese by Ernest George Ravenstein. 1898.

Second Series

1, 2. The Embassy of Sir Thomas Roe to the Court of the Great Mogul, 1615–19. Edited by William Foster. 1899.

9. The Journey of Pedro Teixeira from India to Italy by land. 1604–05. Translated and edited by W. Frederic Sinclair, with additional notes, etc., by Donald William Ferguson. 1901.

12. The Countries round the Bay of Bengal. Edited from an unpublished MS., 1669–79, by Thomas Bowrey; by Col. Sir Richard Carnac Temple. Bart. 1903.

16. John Jourdain's Journal of a Voyage to the East Indies, 1608–17. Edited by William Foster.

17. The Travels of Peter Mundy. Edited from an unpublished MS. by Col. Sir Richard Carnac Temple, Bart. vol. I. 1908.

Extra Series

The Principall Navigations, Voyages, Traffiques, and Discoveries of the English Nation. By Richard Hakluyt, Preacher, and sometime Student of Christ Church in Oxford. James MacLehose and Sons. Glasgow. 1903–05. 12 vols (with index).

HAMILTON, ALEX., CAPT. A New Account of the East Indies. Edinburgh. 1727. Astley, vol. III.

HARLEIAN COLLECTION OF VOYAGES. 2 vols. 1747.

HARRIS, JOHN. Navigantium atque Itinerantium Bibliotheca, or, A Compleat Collection of Voyages and Travels. 2 vols. 1705.

HAVART. Op-en Ondergang van Coromandel. 1693.

HAWKINS, CAPT. W. Relation of the Occurrents . . . in India, 1608–13. Hakluyt, vol. IV; Kerr, vol. VIII; Purchas, vol. I; Thevenot, vol. I. Hak. Soc. Publ. I, 57.

HEDGES, SIR WILLIAM. Diary. Hak. Soc. Publ. I, 74, 75, 78.

HERBERT, SIR THOMAS. A Description of the Persian Monarchy now beinge the Orientall Indyes. 1634. Some Years' Travel into Africa and Asia the Great. 1677. Thevenot, I.

HOFMANN, J. C. Oostindianische Voyage. Cassel. 1680.

HOLDEN, E. S. The Mogul Emperors of Hindustan. 1895.

HOUTMANN, C. Erste Reise nach Ostindien. Allg. Hist. vol. VIII (De Erste Schep Vaert, etc. Amsterdam. 1595).

HUNTER, SIR W. W.
History of British India. London. 1897.
Imperial Gazetteer of India London. 1887.

IBN BATUTA, Travels of, in Asia and Africa. Translated from the abridged Arabic MS copies preserved in the Public Library of Cambridge. London. 1829.

INDIA OFFICE MS. RECORDS.
Factory Records. Miscellaneous, vols II, III, IIIa, and XIV (Diary of Streynsham Master).
The Journal of Peter Mundy.

JORDANUS, FRIAR. Hak. Soc. Publ. I, 31. Receuil de Voyages,* vol. IV.

JOURDAIN, JOHN. Hak. Soc. Publ. II, 16.

KEENE, H.G. Oriental Biographical Dictionary, founded on materials collected by the late Thomas William Beale. A new Edition, revised and enlarged by Henry George Keene. London. 1894.

* See below, *Reccuil de Voyages.*

KERR, ROBERT. A General History and Collection of Voyages and Travels. 18 vols. Edinburgh. 1811–24.

KNOX, J. A new Collection of Voyages, Discoveries, and Travels. 7 vols. [Printed for J. Knox.] 1767

KNOX, ROBERT. Historical Relation of Ceylon. London, 1681.

LAHARPE, J. F. Abrégé de l' Histoire Generale des Voyages (Prevost's). 24 vols. Paris. 1816

LANCASTER, SIR J., Voyage of, to the East Indies. Hak. Soc. Publ. I, 56; Astley, vol. I; Hakluyt, vols II and IV; Purchas, vol. I, etc.

LANE-POOLE, S.

Medieval India under Mohammedan Rule. (" Story of the Nations " Series.) 1903.

Also Article in *Quarterly Review*, vol. CLXXVI, p. 491.

LETELLIER, JEAN. Voyage aux Indes orientales. Dieppe. 1649.

LINGEN, HENRI RUTH DE. Relatio rerum notabilium regni Mogor in Asia ex R. P.. Henrici Ruth de Lingen, Soc. Jesu, . . . narrationibus coram serenissimo duce Newburgino excerpta. Aschaffenburg. 1665.

LINSCHOTEN, J. H. VAN. Voyage of, to the East Indies. Hak. Soc. Publ. I, 70, 71. Astley, vol. I; Purchas, vol. II. (Discourse of Voyages into the East and West Indies, 1598.)

LOPES, DAVID. Chronica des Reis de Bisnaga. Lisbon. 1897.

LOPEZ, THOMÈ. Navigatione verso l'Indie Orientali (1502). Ramusio, vol. I.

LORD, HENRY. A Display of two forraigne Sects in the East Indies. 1630. Churchill, vol. VI.

MAFFEI, J. P. Historiarum indicarum libri XVI selectarum, item ex India epistolarum libri IV. Cologne. 1589.

French translation. Paris. 1665.

MAGISTRIS, PÈRE H. DE. Relation dernière de ce qui s' est passé dans les royaumes de Mandure, de Tanjaor, etc. Paris. 1663

MANDESLO, J. A., Voyage and Travels of, into the East Indies, rendered into English by John Davies of Kidwelly. London. 1669. Harris, vol. I.

MANDEVILLE, SIR JOHN, The Voiage and Travaile of Sir John Maundevile, Kt, which treateth of the Way to Hierusalem, and of Marvayles of Inde. 1725. Hakluyt, ovol. II; Kerr, vol.I; Purchas, vol. III.

MANRIQUE. Itinerario de las missiones del India Oriental. Rome. 1563.

MANUCCI, NICCOLAO. Storia do Mogor. Indian Text Series. 1907. See also above, "Catrou."

MARCO POLO. The Book of Ser Marco Polo. Cordier's edition of Col H. Yule's Translation. 1903.

MARIA, VINCENT. Vincenzo Maria Viaggio all' Indie Orientali. Rome. 1672.

MARSHALL, JOHN. Notes and Observations of East Indies, per John Marshall, 1668–1672. Brit. Museum, MS. Department (Harleian, 4254).

MARTIN, F. Description du Premier Voyage faict aux Indes orientales par les François. 1604 and 1609.

MEMOIRES pour servir a l'histoire des Indes orientales, par M. S. D. R. aris. 1688.

METHOLD, W. Relations of the Kingdome of Golconda, etc. Purchas his Pilgrimage, p.995; Thevenot, vol. I.

MIDDLETON, SIR H. Voyage. Hak. Soc. Publ. I, 19.

MILDENHALL, JOHN. Travailes into the Indies, etc. Purchas, vol. I. Gottfried.

MONIER WILLIAMS, SIR. Modern India and the Indians. Third edition. Trübner's Oriental Series. 1879.

MONTFART, M. DE. Exact and curious survey of all the East Indies. 1615.

MOTTA, ALEXIO DA. Routier pour la navigation des Indes orientales. Thevenot, vol. I.

MUNDY, PETER. See above, "India Office MS. Records." Also Hak. Soc. Publ. II, 17.

MURRAY, HUGH. History of Discoveries and Travels in Asia (vol. II). Edinburgh. 1820.

NIEUHOFF, J. Zee-en Land-Reyze, etc. Amsterdam, 1693. Churchill, vol. II; Astley, vol. III; Pinkerton, vol. VII.

NIEWT. Beschryving door Malabar en Coromandel.
Amsterdam. 1672.

NIKITIN, ATHANASIUS. Hak. Soc. Publ. I, 22.

ORIENTE conquistado a Jesu Christo. 1710.

ORME, ROBT. Historical Fragments of the Mogul Empire.
London, 1782.

OSORIO, JÉRÔME. De rebus Emanuelis Lusitaniae regis virtute et auspiciis gestis, a Hieronymo Osorio.
Lisbon, 1575.
English Translation. 1752.

OVINGTON, J. Voyage to Suratt (1689). London. 1698.
Allg. Hist. vol. x.

PIGAFETTA. Descriptio Indiae orientalis. Frankfort. 1588.

PIMENTA, NICHOLAS. Indian Observations (1597–99).
Purchas, vol. II.

PINKERTON, JOHN. A General Collection of the best and most interesting Voyages and Travels in all parts of the World. 17 vols. 1808–14.

PINTO, F. MENDEZ, Voyage of. English Translation, 1692.
Voyages and Adventures of, Done into English by Henry Cogan, with an introduction by M. Vambéry. Adventure Series. 1891. Purchas, vol. III.

PREMIER LIVRE DE L'HISTOIRE DE LA NAVIGATION AUX INDES ORIENTALES par les Hollandois, par G. W. A. W[illem] L[odewijcksz]. Cornille Nicolas.
Amsterdam. 1609.

PRÉVOST, ABBÉ A. F. Histoire Générale des Voyages.
20 vols. Paris. 1746–89.

PURCHAS, SAMUEL.
Purchas his Pilgrimage; or Relations of the World and the Religions observed in all Ages and Places discovered. The fourth edition, much enlarged with additions, . . . and three whole treatises annexed. London. 1626.
Purchas, his Pilgrimes (Haklytus Posthumus), in four " volumes." Edition in twenty volumes.
Glasgow. 1905–6.

PYRARD DE LAVAL, F. Hak. Soc. Publ. I, 76, 77, 80. Purchas, vol. II; The World Displayed, vol. x.

RAMUSIO, G. B. Delle Navigationi et Viaggi. 3 vols. Venice. 1583–1613.

RECEUIL DE VOYAGES ET DE MEMOIRES publié par la Societé de Geographie. 7 vols. Paris. 1824–44.

RELATION de rebus in India orientali a Patribus Societatis Jesu 1598 et 1599 peractis. Mayence. 1601

RENAUDOT, ABBÉ. Anciennes Relations des Indes et de la Chine. 1718.

ROBERTSON, DR WILLIAM. Historical Works (vol. XI "India").

ROE, SIR THOMAS. The Embassy of, to the Court of the Great Mogul. Hak. Soc. Publ. II, I, 2. Churchill, vol. I; Kerr, vol. IX; Pinkerton, vol. 8; Purchas, vol. I. [Reprinted with Fryer's Travels, Trübner's Oriental Series].

SAAR, J. J. Five years' military service in the East Indies, and account of what happened in the Island of Ceylon, from 1644 to 1659. (In German.) Nuremberg. 1662.

SAINSBURY, NOEL. Calendar of State Papers (Colonial, 1513–1619).

SANTA MARIA, J. Prima speditione all' Indie orientali (1655). Rome. 1661.

SANUTO, MARINO. Liber Secretorum fidelium Crucis super Terrae Sanctæ recuperatione.

SAO, FREY GASPARD DE. Itinerario de India por terra a te esta reine Portugal. Lisbon. 1611.

SCHOUTEN, WOUTER.
Voyage de Gautier Schouten aux Indes Orientales (1658–1665). Traduit du Hollandais. Rouen. 1725.
Thevenot, vol. I. Allg. Hist. vol. XII.

SEWELL, ROBERT. A Forgotten Empire (Vijayanagar). 1900.

STEELE, R. (and J. CROWTHER). Journal of a Journey from Azmere in India, to Spahan in Persia (1615–16). Kerr, vol. IX; Purchas, vol. I.

STEFANO, HIERONIMO DI SANTO. Hak. Soc. Publ. I, 22 Ramusio, vol. I.

STREYNSHAM MASTER. See India Office MS. Records.

TAVERNIER, J. B. The Six Voyages of. Ball's Translation. 1889. Harris, vol. I; Pinkerton, vol. VIII.

TEIXEIRA, PEDRO. Hak. Soc. Publ. II, 9.

TERRY, EDWARD. Voyage to East India. London. 1655. (Reprinted 1777.) Kerr, vol. IX; Purchas, vol. II; Thevenot, vol. I.

THEVENOT, JEAN. Travels into the Levant, i.e., Turkey, Persia, the East Indies. 1687. Harris, vol. II; The World Displayed, vols XI, XII.

THEVENOT, MELCHISEDECH. Relation de divers Voayges (*sic*). Paris. 1683.

TOWNSEND, MEREDITH. Asia and Europe. 3rd edition. London. 1905.

VALENTYN FRANÇOIS. Oud en Nieuw Oost Indien. 5 vols. Amsterdam. 1624.

VALLE, PIETRO DELLA. Hak. Soc. Publ. I, 84, 85. Pinkerton, vol. IX; Thevenot, vol. I.

VARTHEMA, LUDOVICO DI. Hak. Soc. Publ. I, 32. Hakluyt, vol. IV; Kerr, vol. VII; Purchas, vol. II; Ramusio, vol. I.

VINCENT, DEAN WILLIAM.

The Commerce and Navigation of the Ancients in the Indian Ocean. Oxford. 1807.

The Voyage of Nearchus, and the Periplus of the Ægean Sea. Translated. Oxford. 1809.

WITHINGTON, N. Extracts of a Tractate . . . left in the Mogul's Countrey by Capt. Best. Purchas, vol. I.

WORLD DISPLAYED, THE, or, A Curious Collection of Voyages and Travels. 1767–68.

ZIEGENBALG. Account of the Religion and Government Learning, and Economy of the Malabarians. Translated from the High Dutch. London. 1697.

INDEX OF TRAVELLERS

Index